Praise for **Invest and Gr**

Great book for the beginning investor, and solid tips for those with decades of experience! Sanjay instructs us on how to achieve financial freedom by working diligently—step-by-step with tried-and-true methods that simply work. I particularly enjoyed learning about the four-dimensional investment and have added new and effective steps to my own investment process. Many thanks!

Tom Fedro | co-founder, Paragon Software Group Corp.;
best-selling author of *Next Level Selling*

Most investing books (and let's be honest, there are many) are as dry as the desert. Despite my best intentions, I usually trade them for something more interesting before I've finished. But Sanjay's book, *Invest and Grow Rich*, was different—he grabbed my attention immediately when he said that most Indian parents do not share their investing secrets. Intrigued, I gave this book a chance as I'm always looking for new ways to grow my investments. I enjoyed how the author empowers those folks who start with nothing to create a solid financial future for their families. With the crushing educational debt that many people start with these days, Sanjay's book gave me hope for all the upcoming generations.

Mark Nureddine | CEO, Bull Outdoor Products;
best-selling author of *Pocket Mentor*

I would highly recommend Jaybhay's book to anyone seeking to carve out some kind of financial future on their own. Let's face it—many of us start from scratch and have to learn on our own the lessons this author spells out for us. Why not save time and energy and shortcut our way to financial freedom? I know it's a cliché, but this author delivers when he says he can show us how to achieve financial freedom with just $500 a month. I've already started to implement his lessons and am excited about my financial future.

Chris Catranis | CEO, Babylon Telecommunications;
best-selling author of *Disruptive Leadership*

This book is a perfect gift for the self-employed, freelancers, and small-business owners who are focusing on how to run a business profitably for their heirs. Be inspired by someone who not only predicted but also created a winning strategy. Missing a family financial advisor with your best interests in mind? Take this author up on his offer to share his family secrets, and see where it leads!

Ali Razi | founder & CEO, Banc Certified Merchant Services

Sanjay is the kind of author whom you want to call and befriend after you read his book. I appreciate that he felt called to share his hard-earned wisdom to give back to the world. His tips and tricks will make sense for anyone starting out or realizing they're at a point in life where they needed to get busy yesterday. Any businessperson trying to figure out how to fund their life, business, and family needs to read this book and learn these lessons.

Tony White | chairman, enChoice

This book is for several groups of people: those starting alone and will have to do it alone, those young people seeking a strategy for financial success, those looking to buy their first home, those in careers who are unable to start their own business, those small-business owners, and finally those wanting to design their financial future for success. If you fit into any of these groups, then this book will help you learn how to accurately—and positively—design your financial future for you and your heirs. The design elements are easy and apply across different stages in your finances, but you need to get started now. I wish I had read this book when I got started as an employee and began making my adult choices on money.

Bill Bierce | award-winning international
business and technology attorney;
best-selling author of *Smart Business Exits*

Sanjay's book is for anyone wanting to take in some solid investing habits designed to change their financial future for the best. I am sharing this book with all the young people in my life who can benefit from "Uncle" Sanjay's advice. If you've ever wished you were part of a family unit that mentors and helps each other and has the track record to prove they know what they're talking about, then this book is for you!

Kristin Cripps | self-made millionaire,
best-selling author of *Shepreneur*

I was surprised to read the author's discussion around training your mind to invest wisely. I've always considered investments to be a matter of depositing money and receiving income. I feel more inspired than ever to make the mental changes this author suggests, such as mentally changing my spending habits, and obtain the kind of success he has achieved. As the author says, one doesn't need to be a genius to have financial success. Knowing I only need to be dedicated and trained has shifted my outlook entirely.

Kathy Stack | Grafx Design and Digital President/CEO

"With $200 to my name and a useless degree, I hopped on a flight to Bangkok." Who doesn't want to read a story about someone who didn't inherit but rather earned their wealth? Of course, you'll want to know exactly how he did it, and luckily for you, Sanjay is willing to share his story. Looking to save some time and train your way to financial freedom? Check out this book detailing a list of interconnected concepts that you have not read about before.

Mary Feury | President, Altec Systems

Invest and Grow Rich

Achieve Financial Freedom with $500 a Month

Sanjay Jaybhay

Leaders
Press

ISBN (pbk) 978-1-943386-65-9
ISBN (ebook) 978-1-943386-64-2

Library of Congress Control Number: 2020902534

Why I Wrote This Book?

My journey from having only USD 200 in my pockets to becoming a millionaire and achieving financial freedom was not an easy one. I had to go through and overcome various crises in my life to achieve this. But with every crisis I faced, I became wiser and richer.

When my wife was pregnant with our eldest, I was so worried about our baby—her safe, healthy arrival into this world and her future. To me, the prospect of being a father was not only a cause for happiness and joy but also worry.

Being a person with a farsighted vision, I want my child to have a secure financial future even before she's born. The best thing a parent can do for their children is not to give them fish but rather to teach them how to fish. Education will be my best inheritance to my children instead of assets or material things. I don't know if they will follow all my lessons or be interested in learning them. But as a parent, I feel it's my duty to teach them. After going through so much in life, I thought I had learned some valuable lessons and wanted to pass them to my children. These kinds of lessons that one learns after facing a series of hardships are precious and need to be passed on.

I've always considered these concepts I had learned as secrets, which I thought I would only share with my children. I did not want to share my concepts with anybody else, as they were the fruits of my huge sacrifices and hard work. Such secrets are meant to be shared only with my family and loved ones and kept from the outside world. This is what Indian parents would do: they will never share any secret knowledge with others.

But I thought differently. I thought that sharing these concepts with the world would be a good way of giving back to society what it has given me. That said, I've written this book to help people all around the world by teaching them my concepts so that they too can have a secure financial future for themselves and their families.

Who Is This Book For?

nvest and Grow Rich can benefit almost anybody out there who's seeking a way to not only manage their money but also be financially free—which is what matters in the long run. That said, these six groups of people will reap the book's maximum benefits:

The first group consists of people who have started their adult life with nothing or little and are the sole breadwinners of their families. Basically, they are on their own.

Next are the young people who have just finished their education and started working. They have the highest chance of becoming millionaires and financially free if they start compounding early in life. It will be very beneficial if these young people read this book before they receive their first paycheck.

Those who are in their thirties and planning to buy their first home will also find this book delightful. *Invest and Grow Rich* can help them make a better decision before making the biggest purchase of their life.

Moreover, the concepts explained in this book can be helpful for people who are doing jobs and are unable to start a business on their own. Various reasons hold a person back from quitting his job and starting his business. *Invest and Grow Rich* can show them how they can become millionaires and financially free without quitting their job through real estate investments. This is a perfect book for first-time real estate investors.

The same goes with small-business owners, self-employed people, and freelancers, for they too can benefit from the various concepts explained here.

Invest and Grow Rich is also a must-read for both married and soon-to-be married couples. It's a guarantee that couples who follow all the concepts in this book will have fewer disagreements or arguments over money, and that helps make their marriage happier.

Finally, this book is for all who would like to know what their financial future will look like. With the help of simple mathematical calculations, you will learn how to predict your financial future. If your future looks bleak, you can make changes to your present lifestyle or spending and investing habits to change your financial future.

Reading *Invest and Grow Rich* is like traveling into the future and seeing what's going to happen there, then coming back to the present and making better choices to change the future for the better.

What Will You Get From This Book

nvest and Grow Rich will give readers both vision and direction, which are critical factors in taking decisive action toward success. To illustrate how vision and direction work together, let us delve into the following examples:

First, let's talk about the moon landing. The moon has always been visible to people all over the world when it's night. Since the moon was visible to the naked eye, people knew which direction to look for it. With this crystal-clear vision and direction, coupled with tremendous action, Neil Armstrong and his team were able to land exactly on the moon—and not on Mars by mistake.

Now let's see what happens when vision is diminished or unclear: The great explorer Christopher Columbus had a great vision to travel to India. But since India was not visible from Europe to the naked eye—as the technology wasn't that advanced in those days—the direction to go to India was not clear. Though Columbus had a great vision, it became muddled because he had an unclear direction. Despite taking tremendous action and preparation for the voyage to India, having no crystal-clear direction caused Columbus to land in America, over seven thousand miles away from India.

Lastly, let's see what happens when there is no vision at all. In case of a treasure hunt, you have no vision of the treasure. All you have is a direction in the form of a map or a set of clues. Without vision, it's hard to find the treasure, but it's not entirely impossible; it could still be found. In many cases, however, such treasures get lost forever because having only a direction (with no vision) is not enough to find them.

Let me tell you that each of you has a treasure of a million dollars hidden somewhere. You cannot get it because you neither have the vision to see it nor the direction to achieve this goal. In the absence of both vision and direction, taking action becomes very difficult. This is the reason the total population of millionaires today is still less than 1 percent of the global population.

Invest and Grow Rich will give you this vision and direction, which are required to take the appropriate action and increase your chances of becoming millionaires and financially free.

Dedication

This book is inspired by my father. I learned so much from him through witnessing his brave fight with illness and received the best inheritance I could have hoped for—an education.
This book is also for those readers who, like me, have entered their adult life with little or nothing. The sole breadwinners. The ones who are alone and must make the big decisions all by themselves. I hope this book can be a good, useful guide and put you on the right path to achieve the success you desire.

Contents

Introduction

This book isn't just about becoming a millionaire; it's a training program in which I share with you how I trained myself to use money wisely. There are eleven simple concepts explained in these pages that will help you become wiser with your money and build a secure financial future for yourself. They will help you predict and visualize your financial future with just a few simple calculations.

I am providing you with these concepts outlined in simple worksheets that, if applied to your present life, will create a bright financial future.

These concepts are all a direct result of my experiences and have made me not only a millionaire but also financially free. I am convinced that these concepts can do the same for you too. I strongly believe they have the potential to benefit everybody.

Your financial stability and future depend on how you choose to use your money every day. We aren't talking about short-term goals but long-term plans for a secure future.

Just as we need to be trained to do anything, we need to train our minds to use money wisely. I promise you this is something you can learn and apply. I'm not saying it will be easy. It may mean some significant changes in spending habits, but I can promise you that you do not need to be a genius to have financial success. We, ordinary people, need to train ourselves and overcome financial handicaps. But can we do it?

Yes, we can.

Listed Here Are The Eleven Concepts Explained In This Book:

01 ....Doubling Concept

02 .... Necessities, Liabilities, and Assets

03 ....Compounding Your Net Worth

04 ....Leverage

05 .... Good Debt, Bad Debt, and Positive Cash Flow

06 ....Active and Passive Income

07 .... Four-Dimensional Investing

08 ....A Supersize Downsizing

09 ....Risk and Volume

10 ....Financial Freedom

11 ....Beating Inflation

This is it, a training program. A financial boot camp that will force you to use your money wisely, if you want to achieve your financial goals.

By following all these concepts and determining to achieve them, you will automatically be forced to rethink how you use your money and make lifestyle changes to achieve your goals. How you choose to apply these concepts will depend entirely on you.

It was difficult to decide which concept I should explain first. Just as all parts of our body are interconnected and rely on each other, so too are all these concepts. Therefore, I am going to explain them as I learned them and show you how each one depends on the other.

Chapter 1

The First Crisis: The Phone Rings

We weren't "slumdogs," and we weren't "millionaires." My family, the Jaybhays, was firmly established in India's middle class. My dad, Dr. Jaybhay, as he was known in the community, had his own clinic. My mom, Neela Jaybhay, stayed home and took care of my sister and me.

As children, we had everything we could ask for, a stable home with caring parents and a hopeful future. My dad worked hard so that he could provide us with a good life and the best education he could afford.

My dad was extremely strict, especially when it came to education. He expected us to study hard and do well in school. We were expected to attend college so that we could have solid careers and bright futures.

Like many Indian parents, my father and mother sacrificed much to ensure my sister and I were well educated. They conformed to society's norms and paid for our education in its entirety. Like other Indian parents, ours would not allow us to get part-time jobs; they believed it would divert attention from our studies, and our grades would suffer.

Parents who can't afford to pay for their children's education will take out an education loan. Although similar to student loans, it is the parents who pay them, allowing their children to focus only on getting good grades.

You might say, "Lucky for you," but it's just a different sort of stress—the pressure not to waste your parent's money is incredibly high.

So you can imagine my father's disappointment when, after completing a degree in engineering, I chose to find work in a different field.

After all the sacrifices my dad had made to give me a good education and make me an engineer, my degree became worthless.

Out of the blue, I became interested in the trade and export business. My dad was skeptical of my decision, but he nonetheless supported me. Fortunately, in 1992, there were no great jobs for engineers, making the decision to move into a different line of work much easier.

My mom was calm and quiet when I broke the news. If I had expected fireworks and angry words, I was to be disappointed. I suppose my parents knew me well enough to know I was just stubborn enough not to listen to an angry tirade. Not that she would have exploded at me. My mother was happy if we were happy. That day, I decided I couldn't allow my parents to pay my way any longer, not when my way differed so greatly from theirs.

After working in India for almost a year, I got an opportunity to work in Bangkok with an Indian export company through a close friend. Surprisingly, my dad didn't recite any lengthy objections; he put a hand on my shoulder and said, "Son, you are at an age where you can decide your own path. Be an engineer, don't be an engineer—just be in a career that you can enjoy for many years to come."

My younger sister, Minal, watched our discussion with vested interest. As the oldest child, my actions were setting a precedent. I think we were both relieved when my parents accepted my decision.

And so, at twenty-two, with $200 to my name and a useless degree, I hopped on a flight to Bangkok. I was on my own in a foreign land where I hadn't even bothered to learn the language. It was like suddenly becoming an illiterate with a hearing problem. I couldn't understand what I was hearing or reading. I started at an entry-level job with very low pay just to gain experience. To say it was a struggle was a gross understatement.

After a year in Thailand, I had picked up some of the language and had started to adjust to the culture and work environment. Then the phone rang.

I couldn't know before picking up that phone that this one call was about to change the course of my life forever, but looking back, I found it hard to imagine I didn't.

It was my mother. "Sanjay?"

Her voice was shaky, worried. "You must come home right away."

Shaky, worried, but determined. It was the voice my sister and I never disobeyed.

"Why, what is it?"

I was shaking now. It was bad news.

"Just come home, Sanjay. Come right away."

Her urgency sparked something in me. I wanted to reassure her that everything would be fine. But how could I when I didn't know what was wrong?

"I'm coming," I said and heard the phone click. She had hung up.

I called into work and asked for immediate leave, which they gave me, and in a short time, I was on a plane back to India, imagining all sorts of horrors that might await me.

When I arrived home, my family came out to greet me. I breathed a sigh of relief. They were all there, smiling at me, healthy and happy. I reached out to hug my mother and sister, but they pulled back.

"Hug Dad first."

They pushed me toward him. *Why Dad first?* I hugged him, then I hugged my mother and my sister, and they asked me questions about life in Thailand.

When all their chatter had died down, I asked them the question I was nervous to ask: "Why am I here? What's happening?"

My mother tutted, "First, let's have something to eat. I made your favorites."

My family followed me to the dining table, and Mom brought out dish after dish. All my favorites, just like she said. After we ate, she ushered me to my old room. "You've had a long day, and you must be tired. Take a little rest. We can talk later."

It was a relief that it was nothing so urgent that it needed to be discussed the moment I walked through the door, but despite their actions and words, I could see that my family was tired and stressed. Something heavy was weighing on them, and they wouldn't tell me what it was.

It was sometime later when my mother finally called me aside. She sat me down between my father and sister and said, "Your father has a motor-neuron disease."

I nodded slowly, trying to comprehend what that meant. I had never heard of this type of disease before. I studied his face; it looked healthy enough. My eyes ran down his body, and I noticed he was trying to hide his right hand from me. When I thought about it, he hadn't used it at all since I'd arrived. When I really looked, it appeared limp, almost lifeless. "Your hand, Dad!"

He shook his head. "It's nothing, really."

"It's *not* nothing, Dad." Minal chastised. "He can't use it at all, Sanjay. This disease, it paralyzes you. It starts small, but it gets worse."

"You're becoming paralyzed?" All the hope that had been building since my arrival had vanished. My dad was sick. Really sick, with a disease I had never heard of. I took a minute to breathe, settle myself, and comprehend what seemed beyond comprehension. My sister began to cry, and my mom's voice shook as she explained, "We've consulted many doctors, but there is no medicine. There is no cure for this."

Tears spilled over her eyes, and I sat with a lump in my throat, staring at my dad's lifeless hand. When Dad started to weep, I broke down too.

Dad, being a doctor himself, knew exactly what was happening to him. He had done his research. The truth was that his body would continue to deteriorate. His spinal cord and brain stem would quit sending signals to his limbs. Eventually, he would be locked inside his paralyzed body, unable to move, swallow, or express himself in any way. Toward the end, he would lose the ability to breathe on his own. Dad tried his best to keep the gory details from us, but we all knew the result would be death, and there was nothing any of us could do to stop it.

It had started with his fingers on his right hand. He realized he was not able to move them, then slowly his entire hand. He was still working, but if it progressed at the same rate at which it had begun, it wouldn't be long before he wasn't able to work at all.

I suddenly felt the weight of my responsibility. My mother was a housewife, my sister was in college, but I had only just started to really work, and my job paid so little. My father was the only real working member of the family. He was our financial rock. Who would pay the household expenses? Who would pay for my sister's schooling?

Dad had cut down all possible expenses and put all his savings into a fixed deposit account in a bank with the highest rate of interest. In India, there is no social security, social welfare, or employment insurance. My dad had no insurance of any sort that could protect him at a time like this. All expenses and Dad's hospital bills were on us.

We had to rally. We had to survive this terrible crisis. As soon as I understood the situation, I determined to work my hardest and try my best to support my family. I was no longer working just for me. I had responsibilities.

My sister didn't expect a free ride, either. She immediately found a job to help support the family. She was unlike any other student in her class, a working college student, and as every working college student knows, it isn't easy.

My mom would care for my dad. My sister and I would work. I momentarily considered moving back home. But why stay in India and look for work when I already had a secure job overseas? I went back to Thailand with much fear for the future.

Dad's health deteriorated, but he was stubborn. He still wanted to go to work and earn for the family. He had his clinic that wouldn't run without him, so he went there every day. Soon, he could use neither of his hands but still insisted on going. Minal's good friend, Harsha Mulchandani, who was studying to be a doctor, went with him every day. She helped him stay mobile for as long as possible, and my family will be forever in her debt.

Dad fought for as long as he could, but once he lost the use of his legs, he had to close his practice. I hated to see him in this state. My heart ached for him. How much pain must he be in? My whole family suffered with him, but we all knew it was nothing compared to what he was experiencing.

My mother's heart broke as she began to take care of her once-vital husband like she would a newborn baby. When my sister wasn't working or studying, she was helping at home. I felt guilty being so far away, even while knowing this was the best way to support my family.

I worked as much as I could. I would eat cheap and live frugally to save every possible penny to send to my family. As much as I sometimes suffered, I knew it was nothing compared to the suffering of my family.

In a way, I am grateful for the misery. This crisis was a catalyst that changed the way I would think about money for the rest of my life. This book is a result of the strategies I developed due to my family's misfortune. This physical, mental, and emotional crisis was made infinitely worse by our own financial pressures. I was determined that, should I end up in a similar condition to my father, I would find a way to remove the financial burden on my family.

Chapter 2

Doubling

Life had attacked my family, and like a tigress protecting her cubs, I was going to fight back. My dad's situation made me think long and hard about my own. What would happen if I became paralyzed in my old age? The disease destroying my father's health was very likely hereditary. Even if I never inherited his disease, it didn't mean that a similar disability couldn't touch me.

I wanted to think that I had time to worry about that. Years, decades even, before I would ever have to worry about something similar happening to me. But stories kept coming to mind of people in their prime who, through disease or some freak accident, were severely disabled.

Christopher Reeve preyed on my mind. He was Superman. The whole world thought of him that way. A young father, active, good-looking. Then he was thrown from a horse and became paralyzed.

Still, that was a freak accident. Wasn't it? Something that happened to a stranger, thousands of miles away? But then I remembered my friend.

A few years before, a close friend of mine, aged eighteen, was caught in a motorcycle accident. That day, he became immobilized from the waist down. I can only imagine the mental and physical pain he would have gone through in knowing he would be disabled for the rest of his life. Fortunately, his parents could easily provide for his care and rehabilitation.

Christopher Reeve had a career that had made him a multimillionaire. It would be torturous if you had to face a

13

financial crisis in addition to the mental and physical pain. If I were to face that same situation, no one would be able to support me like that. I was on my own.

Friends had all sorts of sage advice. Insurance seemed to be their answer to all unforeseen circumstances. But insurance can protect you only up to a certain age. After that, you are again on your own.

Many insurance companies will only cover you until the age of sixty-five or seventy, and the majority of those consider your medical history for potential risk. I had heard too many horror stories of people whose insurance companies found loopholes in their contracted coverage and failed to pay out. I would not trust my long-term security to a business like that. I had to find security on my own. I had to develop a long-term vision to protect myself as I grew older.

Just as I had watched my father learn to compensate for his handicap, I would learn to compensate for my own deficiencies. Dad had lost the use of his right hand, so he learned to use his left. Then he lost the use of both hands, so he did what he could with his mouth. My father had trained himself to overcome and compensate for his failing health.

They say that if you lose your vision, your sense of hearing becomes more acute. My handicap was financial. Once I recognized this, I learned to develop my "money sense." I hope you don't think me a bighead, but as I write this, I can relate a little to superheroes, like Daredevil. When Daredevil became blind, he realized he could develop his hearing to a superhuman level.

I'm not saying my heightened awareness of money and how to use it is superhuman, but it does seem uncommon these days. Like Daredevil, I developed a training program for myself. I learned how to use my money wisely and build a secure financial future for myself and my family.

At that time in my life, I was financially quite illiterate. When crisis hit, money matters didn't make sense to me, and I was reading things without comprehension. It was like I had felt in those initial days in Thailand. I wasn't completely uneducated. Studying for my engineering degree, I had learned to do fancy mathematical calculations, but I was *financially* uneducated.

It doesn't matter what we are—teachers, doctors, engineers. Any professional can still be financially illiterate. In school, they prepare us to get a job and earn money, but they don't teach us how to manage it. Yes, they may teach you mathematics and accounting, but that does not equal a financial education. To be able to count money and to be able to manage money are two completely different things.

Lesson one was all about learning to look with new eyes and building a long-term vision for myself. Initially, my situation seemed hopeless. I needed to find hope again so that I could cast goals for the future. I believed that I could change things with hard work and determination.

My first step was to build a long-term vision using the concept of *doubling,* and so I created a chart for myself to see the effects of doubling money in the long term. For you to also build this vision, I would like to ask you one question:

If I offered you a choice between $10 million today or $1 that would double every day for thirty-one days, and you would keep the resulting amount, which option would you choose?

I am sure you already know the correct answer, but did you realize that the dollar would double to $1,073,741,824 in one month! Yes, that's right, over a billion dollars in thirty-one days. Seems unbelievable, doesn't it? Don't believe it? Check the chart below.

DOUBLING CHART

DAY		DAY	
1	$1	16	$32,768
2	$2	17	$65,536
3	$4	18	$131,072
4	$8	19	$262,144
5	$16	20	$524,288
6	$32	21	$1,048,576
7	$64	22	$2,097,152
8	$128	23	$4,194,304
9	$256	24	$8,388,608
10	$512	25	$16,777,716
11	$1,024	26	$33,554,432
12	$2,048	27	$67,108,864
13	$4,096	28	$137,217,728
14	$8,192	29	$268,435,456
15	$16,384	30	$536,870,912
		31	$1,073,741,824

If I had said, "Take the dollar doubled every day, and you'll be a billionaire by the end of the month," you might not have believed me. With the chart, you can see it for yourself that it is absolutely true.

Once you see it, once you have that vision, then you know that you can work toward it and take action to make it happen.

To be fair, doubling your money every day would be miraculous. Only God can do it. Not even Warren Buffett can double his money *every day*. This *doubling chart* is only to build a vision. It lets us see the long-term effects of doubling money.

This vision made a huge difference in my life. It gave me hope. I wasn't starting with much, but I had more than a dollar, and I understood that you need money to make money. So if I started to make my money work for me, if I started to find ways to double it, I would soon find my situation improve.

Since the fastest way to double your money is by compounding it, the next important question I asked myself was this one:

At what rate am I compounding my investments?

It wasn't a question I could answer immediately. I was in such a middle-class mindset that I hadn't given much thought to investing for the future. I had one very small investment made from my savings. But was I compounding that investment? No. The investment I had was not compounding; it wasn't able to double its worth.

Compounding works like this: The poor spend all their capital and save nothing. The middle-class invest their savings to make a profit. They then spend the profits, enabling them to preserve their capital. The rich preserve their capital and never spend the profits. They reinvest the profits to earn more profits. This is compounding. [1]

---

[1] For a detailed breakdown of how to compound your investments, please see "Compounding" in the Extra Helps section of this book's appendix.

How the Rich, the Middle-Class, and the Poor View Money

There is a difference in mindsets between the classes that makes all the difference in their financial future.

The rich know the exact rate at which they are compounding their investments, and if they ask themselves at what rate their investments are being compounded, they can answer it without hesitation.

The poor have little awareness of compounding. A person barely scraping by each day has no chance of investing.

The middle-class usually know what compounding is exactly but rarely compound their investments. Why live more frugally just to have more money to invest? I am making a profit on my investments. Isn't that good enough?

The rich not only know exactly what compounding is but also have found a way to do it well, and they follow through with the necessary action.

Action is a major factor. People all over the world saw the moon and shared the same vision to travel there. But who—apart from the Russians and Americans—took action? Who invested their time, money, and energy into making this impossible mission *possible*? The great space race only had two competitors. They turned vision into thought and thought into action.

There are billionaires, like Bill Gates and Mark Zuckerberg, who had great ideas in college and dropped out to achieve them. They couldn't stand the idea of letting any more time stand in the way of acting on their vision. With each goal they achieved, they moved on to another seemingly impossible goal. They compounded their success.

A dollar invested in a way, which, if doubled every day for thirty-one days, would turn into a billion! That was my vision. I had something to set my sights on. Now I could visualize all sorts of possibilities, and my mind began to work on setting a more achievable goal. I wasn't aiming to be a billionaire, but I did want to be financially secure for the future, and I needed to know how much that would take.

> **Assuming investors like Warren Buffett double their money every three years by**
>
> **compounding it at a rate of 25 percent annually, I wondered, could I imitate them as an investment model?**
>
> **Was this realistic for middle class me?**

How could I apply this to my life? I prepared a doubling chart for my own life. With the help of this chart, I was able to predict my own financial future. I wanted to see how much money I would have by retirement. I tell you: this exercise is a wakeup call!

We are likely starting in very different places from one another, so as an experiment, I prepared case studies of four people who start investing from different financial positions.

1 Oliver $1

2 Frank $4,000

3 Thomas $10,000

4 Stephen $65,000

Poor Oliver looks like he's at a terrible disadvantage, but the point is that you can start, even with just $1. (If you don't have even $1, I can assume you have stolen this book, and at a pinch, you could sell it for at least $1.)

Great! So even if you are starting with just $1 (from a stolen book), you have something to invest.

A very low start means that you will need several cycles of doubling your money to reach your goal. For example, if Oliver has a goal to achieve $1 million, and he starts with only $1, then from the doubling chart below, you can see that he needs to double his money twenty times in his lifetime to achieve this target.

Can he do it? Yes, he can!

Doubling Chart

DAY	Oliver	Frank	Thomas	Stephen
1	$1	$4,000	$10,000	$65,000
2	$2	$8,000	$20,000	$130,000
3	$4	$16,000	$40,000	$260,000
4	$8	$32,000	$80,000	$520,00
5	$16	$64,000	$160,000	$1,040,000
6	$32	$128,000	$320,000	
7	$64	$256,000	$640,000	
8	$128	$512,000	$1,280,000	
9	$256	$1,024,000		
10	$512			
11	$1,024			
12	$2,048			
13	$4,096			
14	$8,192			
15	$16,384			
16	$32,768			
17	$65,536			
18	$131,072			
19	$262,144			
20	$524,288			
21	$1,048,576			

Not bad for starting with just one dollar! Imagine if he started out in Frank's position. Frank doesn't have much, but he has managed to save $4,000. That isn't anything to sneeze at. You can see he only needs to double his money eight times to reach $1 million.

The higher the amount you start with, the fewer number of times you will need to double your money to hit that same bank balance. Stephen worked hard and lived frugally, and he managed to save $65,000. This meant that in only four doubling cycles, Stephen had already reached that million-dollar mark.

That's my theory. That was the vision I needed to work toward a goal, but I needed to set my sights on what was achievable. I needed to start using some real-world math to see what my actual financial future would look like.

We are going to use Stephen as an example of what I tried next.

Let's say that Stephen was thirty-five by the time he has saved $65,000. He invests this money with an annual return of 10 percent. That's nothing too crazy, and it certainly isn't doubling every year. The 10% seemed achievable. But would that achievable goal get me to the place I wanted to be by retirement?

In theory, if you can get a 10 percent return compounded on your money, you could double your money in approximately seven years. In seven years, Stephen will double his money, at the age of forty-two. He will double his money once again in seven years, at the age of forty-nine, and so on.

Stephen's Doubling Chart With 10 Percent Return

YEAR 1	YEAR 7	YEAR 14	YEAR 21	YEAR 28
$65,000	$130,000	$260,000	$520,000	$1,040,000
AGE 35	AGE 42	AGE 49	AGE 56	AGE 63

Stephen only needs to double his money four times to become a millionaire. At a 10 percent rate of return, it would take him twenty-eight years. He is thirty-five years old now and saved $65,000 to invest with an annual rate of 10 percent for twenty-eight years, which gives him $1 million by the age of sixty-three.

How he uses his hard-earned money is important. The less he has to invest, the longer it will take to achieve his goal. It's important to note here that Stephen can achieve a million dollars by the age of sixty-three, with only a one-time investment of $65,000 at the age of thirty-five. If he continues to invest his savings every year, beyond the age of thirty-five, this figure will become much bigger.

As I looked at ways to become financially secure, I realized that the key was *saving* and *investing*. If my current lifestyle didn't allow room in my budget to save, it would be difficult for me to invest, and my future was going to be bleak.

As I researched financial planning, training myself to sharpen my money sense, I discovered the *rule of 72*.

Essentially, the rule of 72 is used to estimate the number of years required to double a financial investment.

Rule of 72

If you divide 72 by the compounded rate of return you are getting on your investments (i.e., 10 percent), the result will be the number of years you require to double this investment (72/rate of return = no. of years required to double your money).

If you are anything like the average person, financial lingo may make you nervous. But let me tell you, this concept is quite simple.

Here's how it works. You save $1,000, and because you are a wise, savvy human being, you invest it in something that will give you compound interest. This particular investment has a compounded rate of return of 10 percent every year. In the rule of 72, you take 72 and divide it by the percentage of compound interest you are earning (72/10 = 7.2). So, in just seven years, your investment of $1000, at 10 percent compound interest, will become $2,000.

Simple, right? And so useful too. As soon as I discovered this little formula, it made it so much easier to map out a financial plan for myself. I could literally test potential investments to see if they would get me to my goal.

Chapter 3

Earning Much Is Not Enough to Secure Your Future
Predict Your Financial Future (Part 1)

You could earn $1 million a year, but if you don't include saving and investing in your million-dollar budget, your future will still look bleak. We see it all the time in celebrity culture. Megastars earning megabucks find themselves in mega debt through poor investments and lavish lifestyles.

In 2015, Kanye West famously announced that he was $50 million in debt! His fans were so concerned that they started a *Kickstarter* campaign to help pull him out of debt. His fans, who were by no means pulling in a superior income to Kanye himself, were in a far better financial position than their idol.

In 1996, almost three years after my dad's diagnosis, I was grappling with the effect of the middle-class trappings on my family. My dad had a good career and had cared for us well, but I doubted his savings could cover the extended care that would be required as he sank further into dependency.

His health had deteriorated quickly. Within two years, he was paralyzed from the neck down. Even his tongue had been affected. He had lost his ability to communicate through speech, and doctors warned us that his lungs would be affected next. When he lost his ability to breathe and eat independently, they would place him on life support.

We had no idea how long he would survive. Doctors couldn't help us plan for this eventuality. They couldn't tell us if he would spend days, weeks, or even months in that state. We had heard of cases where patients with the same disease were on life support for years. I knew we could afford to pay for his hospitalization and life support for several months, but if it were to stretch into years...

I began to prepare myself mentally to provide for his care, even if it meant we sell everything we have or borrow money to keep him alive. I couldn't imagine letting my dad die because I didn't have the money for his care. I just couldn't let that happen, and I would never be able to live with myself if I did.

Preparing for my financial future became more important than ever. How could I earn enough to ensure this would never happen to my family or me? The lesson here is obvious: how much you earn is not as important as how much you can save and how you can invest it.

It was during this time that I discovered a way to predict my financial future—based not on how much I earned, but on how much I saved and how I invested my savings.

There were two major elements to this process: the first was predicting how much money I would have at the time of retirement, and the second was what my expenses at retirement would be. Both predictions were essential to knowing if what I saved would be enough.

That is what I want to share with you. I know this part of my story is a bit heavy, and I hope I haven't left you feeling depressed, but I believe my story and these steps I've developed as a result have the power to transform your future the way they did mine.

Ready to predict your own financial future? You may need to get out some recent bank statements to be accurate, but even taking an educated guess will give you some idea. So I've made you a little chart, just the same as the ones I used to figure out my own financial future.

You will notice there is a box marked "rate of return." If you need a little assistance to calculate what your rate of return would be, please refer to the help section, and it will walk you through the (very simple) steps.

Be honest here. This is just for you, your real-life situation.

YOUR FINANCIAL FUTURE - STEP 1

AGE	AMOUNT INVESTED	RATE OF RETURN

(On the off chance that those three blank boxes are intimidating, below is another example that shows how to use this beautifully laid out chart.)

Step 1

THOMAS' FINANCIAL FUTURE - STEP 1

AGE	AMOUNT INVESTED	RATE OF RETURN
35	$10,000	10%

Step 2

Using the rule of 72, we'll look at how many years it will take to double your money. (That's 72/10 = 7.2, so we will make it seven years for easy calculation.)

Step 3

All good so far? Once you know the number of years it will take to double your money, you can calculate from your current age to see how much money you will have by retirement age. (I'm using a median age of sixty-three, since average retirement age worldwide is from sixty to sixty-five,)

Your Doubling Chart, Investing At A Rate of__Percent

YOUR FINANCIAL FUTURE - STEP 3

AGE	Balance
	Investment - $
	End of 1st Cycle - $
	End of 2nd Cycle - $
	End of 3rd Cycle - $
	End of 4th Cycle - $

Thomas's Doubling Chart, Investing At A Rate of 10 Percent

THOMAS' FINANCIAL FUTURE - STEP 3

AGE	Balance
35	Investment - $10,000
42	End of 1st Cycle - $20,000
49	End of 2nd Cycle - $40,000
56	End of 3rd Cycle - $80,000
63	End of 4th Cycle - $160,000

**Stephen's Doubling Chart, Investing
At A Rate of 10 Percent**

STEPHEN'S FINANCIAL FUTURE - STEP 3

AGE	Balance
35	Investment - $65,000
42	End of 1st Cycle - $130,000
49	End of 2nd Cycle - $260,000
56	End of 3rd Cycle - $520,000
63	End of 4th Cycle - $1,040,000

According to the rule of 72, Thomas can expect to have a $160,000 balance by the time he retires.

How does your chart look? Does it surprise you? Let's compare Thomas's and Steven's financial futures. Stephen had the same compounded rate and is the same age as Thomas, but because he is starting with a much larger investment ($65,000), by the time he retires, he will be a millionaire.

If Thomas wants to be at the same place as Stephen by the time they retire, he will either need a much larger investment or a larger rate of return.

It didn't make one iota of difference, to their financial futures, that Thomas was smarter in school, went to a better college, and was more popular with the ladies. Both started in the same company and the same position at the age of twenty-four and earned the same salary. But Thomas spent those early years blowing his budget and spending his full income each month. He wasn't in debt, but he wasn't ahead either.

While Thomas took exotic vacations, Stephen stayed a little closer to home and chose cheaper accommodation. While Thomas got himself an awesome sports cable package and high-speed internet, Stephen opted for a barebones package and spent more time with family and friends, finding fun but free entertainment.

Every month from the time he was twenty-four years old until the age of thirty-five, Stephen managed to save, on average, $500 a month. After eleven years, that gave him a hefty savings of nearly $66,000.

The simple differences in their spending and saving habits meant that Thomas and Stephen had drastically different retirements—Thomas with a mere $160,000 to see him through the coming years, Stephen with over $1,000,000.

Who knew saving $500 a month for eleven years and investing it at a rate of 10 percent return per annum until you're sixty-three would make you a millionaire?

Shall we play with poor Thomas's future a little more? Let's just say that he didn't bother to make any good investments. He just wasn't into the whole "investing thing." Thomas is obviously the kind of guy that wants to live for the moment. He prides himself on it. He travels, eats sushi in Japan, bungee jumps in New Zealand, surfs in Hawaii. He is doing all right, and he just can't be bothered to take the time out of his busy day to figure out what makes a good investment. But he's smart enough to know he needs to save a little for the future, so he deposits his savings in the bank at an interest rate of 2 percent per year and makes sure never to dip into those savings no matter what.

What happens to Thomas's financial future now? Let's try out the rule of 72 again:

72/2 percent = 36. It will take thirty-six years for Thomas to double his money. So at the age of seventy-one, that $10,000 in savings will become a $20,000 balance. Now we see a massive difference in Thomas and Steven's doubling charts.

THOMAS' DOUBLING CHART		STEPHEN'S DOUBLING CHART	
AGE	2% RETURNS	AGE	10% RETURNS
35	$10,000	35	$65,000
42	----------	42	$130,000
49	----------	49	$260,000
56	----------	56	$520,000
63	$17,410	63	$1,040,000.00
70	----------	70	$2,080,000.00
71	$20,000	71	$2,288,000.00

It sounded good at the time. Thomas thought he was being frugal, taking that $10,000 in savings and putting it in a savings account. But by the time these two old friends are seventy-one, it looks like Stephen has won the lottery, and Thomas is reduced to scraping by on his pension and his small amount of savings. If anything unforeseen should crop up, Thomas is in serious trouble.

While Thomas was busy posting his travel exploits on *Facebook*, Stephen was making his first and most important financial decision. He would save enough to have a great down payment on a property or on a solid investment with good returns.

It's a bit of a wake-up call, isn't it? At least, it was for me. My dad was in Thomas's position. He had made a decent income as a doctor, and we lived well, but now we were struggling. Dad was in a wheelchair, and medical bills and daily expenses would have eaten up any savings he had if I was not there to support my family. I needed to do all I could to provide for my family. I needed to be a Stephen.

I recognized there were two important questions that would determine my financial future:

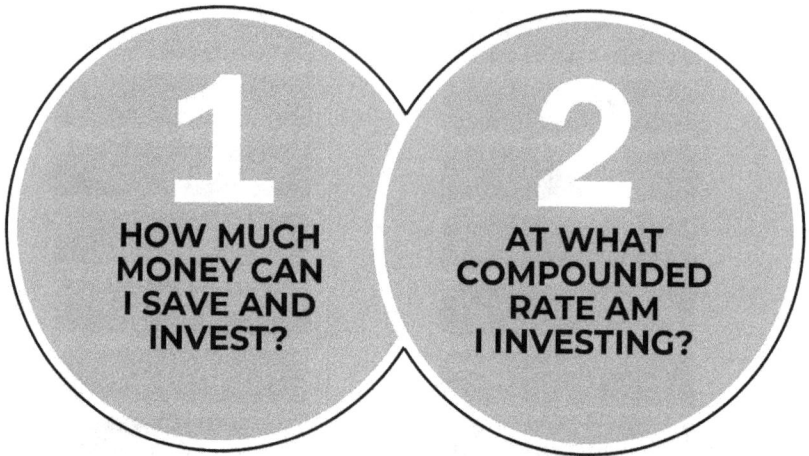

Large investment + high rate of return = achieving goals very quickly.

Small investment + small rate of return = goals taking more time than you have.

Was I ambitious enough to achieve these higher goals? How much was that secure future worth to me? Was I willing to give up a cushy lifestyle now to have peace of mind in my retirement? How high could I aim? If I wanted to be a billionaire by retirement age, I would need to invest a much higher amount. In fact, the difference between hitting the billion-dollar mark and the million-dollar-mark is three zeros. If Stephen could have invested $65,000,000 by thirty-five at a compounded rate of 10 percent, he would quite easily be a billionaire by sixty-three.

Obviously, if you have $65,000,000 by thirty-five, you have already graduated from this program. So, instead, let's say that your rate of return is much higher. Let's say 25 percent, like Warren Buffet in my earlier assumptions. Applying the rule of 72 shows us that it would take almost three years to double your investment (72/25% = 2.88).

We're going to round it to three years to simplify things. Your money is doubled in three years. Sounds pretty good, doesn't it? And this time, just for fun, let's start at our "out there" goal of $1 billion to see at what age we would need to have that $65,000.

DOUBLING CHART

BACKWARDS FROM BILLIONAIRE		BACKWARDS FROM MILLIONAIRE	
AGE		AGE	
63	$1,000,000,000	63	$1,000,000.00
60	$500,000,000	60	$500,000.00
57	$250,000,000	57	$250,000.00
54	$125,000,000	54	$125,000.00
51	$62,500,000	51	$62,500.00
48	$31,250,000	48	$31,250.00
45	$15,625,000	45	$15,625.00
42	$7,812,500	42	$7,812.50
39	$3,906,250	39	$3,906.25
36	$1,952,125	36	$1,953.12
33	$976,562.50	33	$976.56
30	$488,281.25	30	$488.28
27	$244,140.62	27	$244.14
24	$122,070.31	24	$122.07
21	$61,035.15	21	$61.03

All right, so this is much better. You don't need to have $65 million by thirty-five to be a billionaire, but you do need almost $2 million. In fact, you would need to have that $61,000 by the time you were twenty-one.

These charts aren't meant to make you feel like you have failed if you aren't there yet. They're really about casting vision. They are just to help us understand the concepts and hopefully be a catalyst for a lifestyle change. We're not aiming to be billionaires; we are aiming for security. We aim to learn these concepts and make them active in our lives.

If you are still young and can start at the age of twenty-one to invest $61.03 at a compounded rate of 25 percent per year, you can be a millionaire by the age of sixty-three. That $61.03 is not even a day's wage working at McDonald's!

$61.03 + ability and capability to invest at rate of 25 percent per year

= $1,000,000 by the time you are sixty-three!

Imagine that. You don't need to start big, but the "younger you" can start, and the greater your return, the higher you can set that goal. How many times have we wasted sixty dollars on stuff we don't really need? One night out to dinner and the movies with friends can cost you that much. Buying a few movies or one video game will cost you that much. How often have you wasted that much money on things that offer very temporary enjoyment?

I know I don't have enough fingers or toes to count the many times I have wasted money this way. I needed to learn the value of those dollars. My dad's health issues were just the start of relearning how to handle my money responsibly. Each one of us has a different situation. We all need to work within the reality in which we live. But each one of us can take steps toward a better financial future.

And since we're casting vision, why not reach for the stars? Without immense vision, humanity wouldn't even have made it to the moon, but now look at how far we've come. Space stations, satellites, Mars rovers, and pictures from Pluto. Imagine what you can do with your salary if you start early. Imagine what our kids could do if we teach them these concepts.

Okay, yes. Finding an investment that would give a 25 percent return on your money every year is extremely difficult. But the concepts are still sound. What we are doing is changing our money mindset. We are building and training our money sense.

(And with a few years of real-life investment under my belt, I can tell you that it is possible to get even higher rates of return than 25 percent a year. But you'll have to wait for a few chapters until we get to the concept of leverage before I tell you how.)

Be warned. It is incredibly easy to fall back into bad spending habits. It is easier to put momentary desires above things that will benefit you twenty or so years in the future. In the beginning, it is a constant wrestle with yourself to choose future security over instant gratification. I want security in my future, but I also want to go out to dinner and a movie with friends. What's thirty dollars, really? It is so easy to justify those expenditures, but if that is not in your budget, it is much better to find a less expensive form of entertainment.

My dad's health continued to worsen. I helped as much as I could from afar, but the burden of his care fell heavily on my mother and sister. Calls from home were always answered with a sense of foreboding. There were hopeful days, of course—odd moments where my dad seemed a little better than the day before—but they were few and far between. I wanted my dad to be with us for as long as possible, but for his sake, I prayed that he wouldn't suffer too much longer.

I had just got home from work when the call came.

"He's gone."

He had passed away peacefully at home. I think that Dad must have prayed and asked God to take him. He knew that if he needed a tracheostomy, ventilator, and feeding tube, it meant being admitted in long-term care. We would have to watch as his quality of life continued to deteriorate, and it would cause us all so much anguish. It's not that my dad shied away from suffering, but he really didn't like being a burden.

35

I tell you my story as a reminder that nobody knows when a crisis will strike, but we can be prepared. If you live in a place prone to tornados, you build a shelter to ride out the storm. If you live in a place prone to earthquakes, you build homes that can better withstand them. The truth of life is that crisis will come, and when it does, we should be prepared.

My dad's illness achieved something significant in my life, and I count it as a blessing. For the first time, I was focused on something other than today. I had developed a long-term vision and had real solid goals for my future.

The first step in achieving my goal is to save and invest. I didn't want just to invest the meager amount in my bank account; I wanted to invest the maximum amount I could. Did that mean I should find another job? Did I need a second income? Should I start my own business? Was that even feasible in the current market? Did I need to make changes to my spending and saving habits?

There were just so many questions to answer.

Chapter 4

Necessities, Liabilities, and Assets

We can moan and groan about the surprises life throws at us. I have done my fair share of that. But if we focus on what we have lost, we will never be able to gain. It was clear to me that unless I did something about it, my financial future was bleak. I realized I could decide for myself the kind of life I wanted to live. I didn't have to let circumstances direct my path. I needed to make choices that would facilitate the financially secure future I desired.

My father's death ended a chapter in my life. I had gained a lot of insights during that time and found that to have financial security, I had two options. One was to increase my income, and the other was to increase my savings and investments. Choosing to pursue one or both these options depended on my capabilities.

Increasing your income depends heavily on your ability. So to understand myself and my abilities became very important. I could easily see examples of others who had made millions by capitalizing on their strengths. Some of these people often seemed uneducated or unwise in many aspects of their lives. They made bad investments, trusted the wrong people to handle their money, or spent more than they made. But they had gotten one important thing right: they worked hard to use their talents and abilities. I felt that if they could do it, I could do it too.

Michael Jackson, for example. Could I learn anything from his success? He didn't always seem to be the sharpest tool in the shed. Tabloids loved to point out all the poor decisions he made in his lifetime. But he had a talent that he developed, and that made him millions. Could I sing and dance like Michael Jackson? I did the moon walk pretty well when I was in school, but my ability to dance and sing, no matter how I worked at it, would never compare to those with real talent. So I had to let go of that option.

Analyzing my capabilities was a little humbling. It's not often that we sit down and take an honest look at our talents or skill set. One thing I learned about myself is that I am a pretty good visionary. I can think of all sorts of ways to make life better. However, I often lack the technical ability to carry my ideas from vision to reality.

I had to ask myself if I even had the ability to develop a life-changing application like *Facebook*, *Airbnb*, or *Uber*. Find an investor, make it successful, and sell it for millions, or list it on the stock exchange. Could I do that? I doubted it. I was just an average guy.

Once I came to terms with the fact that I was just an average guy without any special talents, my options became narrower. I looked at the option of starting a traditional business in Bangkok, a trading company, a restaurant, or a factory. But all these traditional businesses needed capital that I did not have.

Starting with only $200, I have no way of opening a business on my own. My options were reduced to finding a better-paying job or an additional job. A better-paying job, if I could find one, was a much better option in my mind. I did my homework and applied to similar jobs that would offer better pay. Fortunately, the homework paid off, and I found one.

Since the only real option I had at that point had been to find a better-paying job, saving my hard-earned money became much more important. To be financially successful, I would have to work at both options together. Increasing my income was a start, but now I had to look at how I should save and invest.

The first step to creating a savings and investing program for myself was to honestly assess the liabilities and assets in my life. I needed to think long and hard over what I considered a necessity and those things that were luxury items. I wholeheartedly believe that this step is crucial to everything else that follows.

You may have heard of the "simplify" trend that is happening now all over North America. Conferences are being held in all the major cities. They deal specifically with helping people recognize the clutter in their lives that is keeping them from living in freedom. We can get so tied down by "stuff."

In America and many countries around the world, people are living with all the luxury items that only belonged to the rich and powerful decades ago. However, they seem less happy than the previous generations. The simplify trend is focused on ridding ourselves of the material things that tie us down. Things that, in theory, should cause us joy and create free time, but, in reality, cause us stress. Amassing "stuff" often steals joy rather than giving it.

On that note, let's take some time and assess the things in your life that are necessities, liabilities, and assets. On the next page, we have a chart for you to fill in. Think carefully about what you believe to be your current assets. Then think about what you have that is a liability. Then in the third column, list those things you believe are necessities at the moment. Remember that some things that are necessities at one point in your life may no longer be necessary in another season. Think honestly about them. It doesn't do us any good if we lie to ourselves about our current situation.

NECESSITIES	LIABILITIES	ASSETS
Necessities are basic needs like food, clothing, shelter, education, and medical care.	A liability is any debt you are currently owing or anything you buy that decreases in value after purchase.	An asset is anything you buy that increases in value after purchase or that can generate cash flow.

Necessities

We all have necessities, things we need to survive. Food, clothing, shelter, education, and medical care are essential, and none of these come for free.

If you happen to be living below the poverty line, all your income is spent on buying necessities, which sometimes won't even be enough to cover these basic needs. In which case, you will need to borrow. When you can't prove that you can easily pay it back, the loan becomes "high risk," and high-risk loans mean high-interest rates for the borrower.

The next month, no matter how much you try to pay back the loan, it is likely that you will have barely enough to pay back the interest. Then you will be tempted to take out a new loan to pay back the debts. This puts you into a vicious cycle of debt. Even if you were able to pay off the debt, there are still necessities every month, which cannot go away.

For many in this cycle, income doesn't increase, but the price of necessities keeps going up. The poor become poorer and cannot dig themselves out of this "necessity hole." If this is where you find yourself, have hope! Fortunately, in many western countries, there are a variety of social services to help you—not only to pull out of debt, but also to gain an education that will put you in a better position to find employment at a higher rate of pay.

These services also can connect you with grant money to start a small business, as well as business courses you get paid to take. They can help you with consolidating loans at lower interest rates. If you find yourself in debt, with no hope of pulling out, you owe it to yourself to do a little homework and find a way to make the system work for you. But remember, once your income increases, don't then fall into the trap and start spending the extra money.

Save and invest whatever you can.

When it comes to necessities, it is important to remember that they tend to grow as our income grows. When we get our first car, we will also need to pay for registration, insurance, fuel, and maintenance. These become ongoing necessities. When we buy our first home, we will begin paying property tax, homeowners insurance, and all sorts of hidden bills. These are also necessities.

As your income grows, you will notice that things you once did without will soon become necessary.

Many people fall into this trap unconsciously. If their income increases threefold, their necessities follow suit. You will find yourself justifying expenditures as necessities that you would have called luxuries before. It is a trick of the mind. Some of our necessities are attached to liabilities. Registration and insurance are necessary when you own a boat. But is the boat a liability? What necessities do you have that are attached to liabilities?

It's hard not to spend money when you have extra, but if you don't make a budget and stick to it, you will find yourself easily blowing all your income on things you have convinced yourself are necessary to your new way of life. Some things will be, like taxes, insurance, and so on, but the temptation will be to buy the bigger house, the more expensive car, and the brand-name wardrobe.

When this happens, you are significantly decreasing your assets by spending money on liabilities. As a result, you will have less money to invest and affect the "doubling process" we talked about in the previous chapter.

After I found a higher-paying job, my income increased, but I did not increase my expenses. I lived in a modest studio in the suburbs of Bangkok and continued to live there to keep my expenses the same and increase my savings.

Have another look at the chart you just filled out. Are there any necessities that you wrote down that may be liabilities? Are there things on the list that are more wants than needs?

Be honest with yourself. If you find your inner lawyer working to justify some of them, then I can guarantee they are not necessities.

As I worked on my own lists, I realized that to invest wisely now, I needed to train myself to spend only on my needs and save and invest the rest.

Liabilities

The middle-class spend most of their money on liabilities. We love the luxuries that a decent income affords us. We buy "reliable" vehicles, which usually means something new, and with a warranty.

The warranty is useful, but that new car depreciates the minute you drive it off the lot. We fill our homes with kitchen gadgets, computers, laptops, and gaming consoles. We spend money on great cable packages, *Netflix*, and high-speed internet. These things are enjoyable, and they give us a false sense of success. Their value is either momentary or declining.

Brand-name clothes, purses, watches, cars, and expensive vacations are all liabilities. The day we buy them, their value decreases, and continues to decrease with time.

Remember the examples of Thomas and Steven? If you flip back to their doubling charts, you can see again the difference in their financial futures based solely on their lifestyle choices.

Let's take a minute to talk about cars. A car is arguably a necessary liability, but the type of car you buy determines how major a loss you are incurring. If you must borrow money from the bank to buy it, then the interest becomes an additional liability.

It's like a double-edged sword, cutting your cash flow from both sides—the bigger and fancier the car, the larger the liability. Car ownership is like reverse compounding. The fastest way to halve your assets is to buy a fancy car.

If your situation in life necessitates having a car, buy an inexpensive one, consider in advance its fuel efficiency, and read up on customer reviews and common problems. As much as possible, try to reduce its liability. If you are a business owner, buy it through your company so that you can claim depreciation.

Most of us would consider a house as an asset—which can be true, but only if we have done our homework. When we buy houses with a big price tag, we open ourselves up to higher interest costs and taxes and costlier maintenance. In the long term, this house can be an asset. Its value will increase, and you won't be wasting money on rent. However, this same house can be a liability if it is too big.

The larger your mortgage, the more you will be paying in interest. It is highly likely that you will pay as much interest over the years as on the original purchase price. All that money spent on interest is money you can't invest. Later in this book, we will work on a doubling chart for your home. If you are currently a homeowner, we will look at how that investment is paying off. If you are looking into purchasing your first home, we will look at some of the issues that should be considered as you take that all-important step.

Do I sound like a party pooper? Well, let me give you a little bit of a break. Once you have looked at your investment opportunities and have created a financial plan based on the predicting-your-financial-future charts, you may find that at sixty or sixty-five, you will be doing quite well. Once you have invested and those investments have started to pay off, you may find that you do have room in your budget for luxuries. By all means, enjoy them! We do not need to live with a poverty mentality, but we do want to live with wisdom.

I honestly can't stress enough how important predicting my financial future was for making big changes in my life. There are so many things in life that we can't plan for, but a retirement fund isn't one of them.

All this advice is, of course, for those of us who are poor or middle-class. To those of us who don't have rich parents who will pay for our liabilities, we are on our own, and we need to be careful about how we use and spend our money.

I can tell you from experience that after learning and putting into practice all the concepts I am sharing with you, you can be a self-made millionaire. No matter your current financial status, without financial education, it is easy to blow all our money on liabilities and find ourselves with a future that is no longer secure.

Assets

Finally, a positive note. Assets are anything we own that increases in value. For example, stocks and properties are assets because they almost always go up in value over time. Yes, they can go down in value too, but if you hold on through the dips, they almost always rise again.

Money in the bank is also an asset, but even cash can devalue due to inflation and national instability. Owning a business is also an asset as its value can increase, and if managed well, it will generate cash flow.

To have the same mentality as the rich, we need to focus our financial plans on acquiring assets. The rich spend money on necessities and liabilities—that is inevitable—but their greater focus will always be on acquiring assets. That is why they are rich.

Take a minute to think about how you have spent your money in the past. Have you ever bought anything that's value increased after you purchased it?

Take a little walk down memory lane, and make yourself a little list. Have you bought any assets?

Then check the chart we filled out earlier. Have you put anything in the assets column?

> **I hate to break it to you, but if you have never bought an asset in your life, you are poor. If your home is your only asset, you are middle-class. If you have bought other assets, besides your primary home, you are rich—or well, on your way to becoming rich.**

If you find that you have blown most of your money buying liabilities, now is the time to start thinking about how you are going to change your spending habits. I can teach you all that I know, but if you don't start to use the knowledge, it will do nothing for your future. So let me help you with a little kick in the pants.

Now is the time to change your spending habits. Now is the moment to think about the changes that you need to make to have money to invest in assets. Just like the poor struggling to dig themselves out of the necessity hole, the middle-class also struggle to pull themselves out of the liability hole.

So here is the first step and my challenge for you.

This month, or even just this week, if you need to take baby steps, cut back your spending on liabilities. No extra clothes or shoes you will only wear once. If the shirt you tried on is not better than every other shirt currently in your wardrobe, do you really need it? Those sunglasses you like that are on sale, will they really add that much to your current lifestyle? Can you buy a generic brand rather than a name brand?

I know you need to live life, but we can all cut some corners. The more money you can save, the more you can invest. Every day, when you take money out of your pocket or hand over that little piece of plastic, ask yourself, "What you are spending it on? Is it a necessity? A liability? An asset?"

If it is a necessity, then go for it. If it is an asset, it is definitely worth it. But if it is a liability, think long and hard over whether it will be worth it to you tomorrow.

A friend of mine, when purchasing clothes, uses this trick. If it is not for an important occasion, she asks herself, "Will I wear it at least once for every dollar I spend on it?" If not, she leaves it at the store. It is a simple way to assess the worth of the liability. Some liabilities will still be of value, but some will cause you more headaches than they are worth.

A better suggestion for most of us, if we can manage it, is to find ways to increase our income rather than compromising our lifestyles. As I mentioned before, you can find a higher-paying job. This may mean changing companies or possibly relocating. You can find an additional job. It is increasingly common, in much of the west, for people to have more than one job.

Or you may find that you have unique skills and the ability to run a business, and it would be worthwhile to quit your current job and start your own business. If, however, you are unable to do any of these things, your only true recourse is to cut spending.

Like I mentioned before, I don't want to be a party pooper or take the fun out of your life, but to have a secure financial future, cutting spending is necessary. It is good practice to earn first, spend later.

Chapter 5

The Second Crisis
The Middle-Class Trap

I t was a new chapter in my life. I had a new job with a better income. My larger paycheck allowed for larger savings. My focus began to shift from financial survival to the bright future ahead. I was on track for the financial security I craved, and then I turned on the news.

They were calling it the "Tom Yum Goong crisis." Overnight, the Thai baht had collapsed. The government had been trying to float the currency so that it could retain crucial ties with the American dollar, but in early July 1997, they found themselves bankrupt.

The baht's value against the USD was cut in half. This meant my savings were half of what they were compared to the dollar. It was a hard blow. I had been so frugal. I had denied myself so much, but my efforts now seemed fruitless.

As the days and weeks passed, the full extent of the crisis began to sink in. I was paid in Thai baht. My increased salary was now also half of what it had been before the collapse. Banks were closing. Large companies and some of Asia's richest families were heading for bankruptcy. Even the Thai government was forced to take a huge loan from the International Monetary Fund (IMF) to survive.

It's hard not to wallow in self-pity when things like this happened. I was in a situation that was completely beyond my control. I asked myself what I could do to survive this. That question helped me shift my focus. I realized that, although my bank account was worth half of what it was a short time before, the baht wasn't the only thing to devalue.

Property prices had crashed to one-third of what they had been. People needed to sell property, but no one was buying. People were afraid to spend on anything. I pushed back my fear and found opportunity. Now was the perfect time to buy.

I gathered my courage, and at the age of twenty-eight, I used my savings on a down payment for a three-bedroom condo. While my friends continued to spend their money on liabilities and expensive vacations, I had been able to save up enough money to buy an asset in one of the most upscale locations in downtown Bangkok.

Top Tip

Watch for these types of down markets. Invest when others are pulling out. Many people waste the opportunity to buy assets during a crisis because they spend their money on liabilities and don't have enough savings to take advantage of a buyer's market.

Don't think I am saying you need to wait for a crisis to buy an asset. That isn't what I mean at all. Any time is the right time to buy an asset, but having some savings will enable you to buy when opportunities like this arise. If you aren't prepared, your dream life will pass you by.

I was fortunate that, due to what I had learned during my dad's illness, I understood the difference between necessities, liabilities, and assets. I had saved money, and I was in the right position to take advantage of the opportunity as it presented itself to me.

Take a little time to think about where your passions lie. The things that are constantly on our hearts and minds are much easier to pursue than things we have only a moderate interest in. Our focus dictates our actions. If your focus is on travel, you will often talk about travel, and most of your savings will be dedicated to your next trip. The result will be a lot of travel. If your focus is on shopping, your focus and your savings will be dedicated to shopping. The result will be a house full of purchases.

Believe me, buying liabilities provides only momentary pleasure. Buying an asset can provide you with long-term enjoyment. An asset can potentially outlive you and provide pleasure even for your children or grandchildren. Whatever you focus on will become a natural and easy part of your life.

If you shift your focus to financial security and plan to buy assets, it will be reflected in your conversations. Your time and your savings will be dedicated to buying assets. It is inevitable that in short order, you will have increased assets and higher net worth.

An added benefit is that those assets will eventually provide you with the opportunity to explore and enjoy other passions. Assets first, travel and shopping later. Financial matters may not be a natural passion. For many people, budgeting and managing personal finances feels more like a necessary evil. But I have found that when we discover the importance of something, we can start to manufacture the interest.

I focused on putting the maximum amount of money into the process of doubling and compounding, and that focus paid off. My assets grew. As my assets grew, so did my interest in growing them.

My life changed the moment I took possession of the condo. I moved out of my little rented studio in the suburbs to my three-bedroom living in the heart of Bangkok. A luxury condo with every imaginable amenity. I wasn't living in a massive penthouse with a private swimming pool and private squash court, but coming from my modest studio, it felt as if I had made it.

Aged twenty-eight, single, and living alone in three-bedroom luxury. You can guess what happened next. Pool parties, clubbing, partying with friends. Bangkok had me. For the first time, after a lot of struggle, I was feeling rich and enjoying life. That was a problem.

Feeling rich and being rich are two very different things. When I predicted my financial future with my savings and investments, it showed me a bright future. But after buying the condo, I tried to predict my financial future again, and it showed me a completely different picture. To understand what happened, I think I first need to explain what net worth is.

I'd like to suggest that there are two definitions of net worth. One is what I call the "feeling rich" definition, and the other is the "really rich" definition of net worth. An individual's net worth is basically his assets minus his liabilities.

In this chapter, we are going to look at both definitions of net worth and study their difference. Let's use Stephen as our example once again. We're going to add up all his assets and liabilities and then subtract the total liabilities from the total assets. This is just an example to understand net worth.

Stephen's "Feeling Rich" Net Worth

Assets	
Present value of Stephen's home	$650,000
Present value of investments in the stock market	$50,000
Cash in bank	$40,000
Present value of car	$40,000
Total assets	$780,000

Liabilities	
Home mortgage	$450,000
Credit card debt	$4,000
Car mortgage	$30,000
Total liabilities	$484,000

"Feeling rich" net worth (assets – liabilities) $780,000 - $484,000 = $296,000

This example of "feeling rich" net worth is borrowed from how a bank might calculate what they could retrieve from you if you cannot pay your debt. It is all your possessions they could sell at their present value so that they can recover their money. In this instance, Stephen is doing all right. He has a little left, though he does have some significant liabilities.

I thought I was doing well also. Life in Bangkok was good. I had started to speak Thai almost like a native. Work was going well, and since I was in the export business, I traveled all around the globe to develop business ties for the company. I became a little addicted to traveling. I went to forty countries on business and ten more for the fun of it.

It was then that I started to forget the lessons I had learned. I started to spend freely. I thought I was just "living life." I considered myself rather successful. I had a car and a great home, both of which I considered assets at the time, and a life that many friends envied. I was falling into a financial abyss. I was losing focus. My present comfort lured me away from my desire for future security.

It's hard to pinpoint the best way to avoid the trap without looking at the differences in the two types of net worth.

The difference between the definition of the "feeling rich" net worth and the "really rich" definition is that "feeling rich" considers your primary home as an asset, even a car may be claimed as an asset as it has some value. The "really rich" definition does not consider neither your primary home nor your car as an asset.

These days, I use the "really rich" definition to calculate my net worth because it is a more accurate representation of true assets. In retirement, we will still need a primary home. Even if you downsize, a portion of that equity will need to be reinvested into a new home. This is why I suggest you calculate your net worth using the "really rich" definition. In fact, a fun exercise might be to calculate your net worth both ways and see the difference.

Look back at your assets, necessities, and liabilities chart. Now, besides assets and liabilities, write down their values, and use this to calculate your "feeling rich" net worth. How does that feel? Do you have a positive net worth? I do hope so, because the next one isn't going to get any better.

Let's look at Stephen's example again, this time with the "really rich" net worth calculation.

Stephen's "Really Rich" Net Worth

Assets	
Equity in his home	$200,000
Investments in the stock market	$50,000
Cash in bank	$40,000
Total assets	$290,000

Liabilities	
Home Mortgage	$450,000
Credit card debt	$4,000
Car Loan	$30,000
Total liabilities	$484,000

"Really rich" net worth (assets – liabilities) $290,000 - $484,000 = –$194,000

In this example, Stephen's real net worth is –$194,000. That is in the negative! Less than zero!

To be honest, since the equity is in the primary home, I wouldn't normally even count this $200,000 equity. I left it in our calculations so that they wouldn't look quite so hopeless. But in effect, Stephen would be bankrupt.

It seems to me that if your net worth is in the negative, you are technically in a more precarious financial position than a homeless person. At least their net worth is zero; yours is below zero. Being in this negative state of net worth is what I lovingly call *"the middle-class trap."* This is what is keeping you from being a millionaire.

Compounding Your Net Worth

We have seen from the doubling charts that if you start to double your money with a meager amount, you will need many more cycles to reach that million-dollar mark. Like Thomas, who started with $10,000 and still ended up without enough money for retirement.

Now Stephen is starting out with almost $200,000 in the red! It will take him a lot of time to get to zero before he can start doubling his money and hit that million-dollar mark. This isn't chump change. He is deep in the hole. Of course, he already has $50,000 in the stock market, which will help him achieve that million-dollar figure, but if he had less debt, he could reach it so much faster, and he might be able to retire sooner.

I hope I haven't frightened you. I don't want you to give up. Remember, this is just a concept. The main point I want to make is that the bigger the home you buy for your personal living, the greater the negative net worth and the deeper the middle-class trap is. So choose the budget for your home carefully. The smaller the trap, the faster you can get out of it.

Some of you may still argue that since Steven had $200,000 of equity in his home, his net worth could not be less than that of a homeless person. To that, I would answer with this principle, my mantra for a happy life: "Always move forward."

Let me give you some examples. I don't want to buy a BMW, drive it for a few years, and then trade it in for a Toyota. Nor do I want to buy a Toyota and, after a few years, sell it to buy a Moped. I don't want to buy a huge four-bedroom home in a great neighborhood and then sell it after a few years to move into a two-bedroom apartment. I don't want to travel business class when I am young and economy class when I get old. Those are all big steps backward.

Believe me, once you choose to upgrade yourself to a certain standard of living, it is incredibly hard to go back. Choose well before you decide on those upgrades. If it can't be a permanent thing, don't do it. You should be able to afford to maintain your chosen lifestyle right up until you die.

This is the reason I don't consider a primary home and car as an asset. You have upgraded yourself to this lifestyle, and it is highly unlikely that you can sell it and go back to a rented apartment or public transport unless there is a crisis.

Already at the bottom, the homeless person can't go down anymore. There is a small possibility that he has become comfortable in his current position, but there is still a chance for him to go forward.

I know from experience how difficult it is to downgrade. It means embracing the discomfort that this causes, and it is even harder if you have a family. Trust me, you don't want to go backward.

Since a home is the biggest expense of a person's life, we must choose wisely. Choose something that is comfortable, but remember that choosing something well below the mortgage your bank allows will benefit you and keep you from having a negative net worth. Negative net worth equals less money to invest in the doubling process.

Many people, after they have paid off the mortgage on their primary home, buy a vacation home. Remember, vacation homes won't be added to your net worth (this is a chosen lifestyle upgrade), and if you have borrowed to buy a vacation home, then you will be in a negative net worth state for a very long time.

The bigger the home, the bigger the trap!

Remember Michael Jackson's Neverland Ranch? Michael was making millions every year, but he kept buying liabilities. His Neverland Ranch home became a major liability; on many occasions, he was in a massive debt because of it.

The negative net worth of the "feeling rich" takes ages to climb out from and will adversely affect their financial future. The faster a person can get out of this middle-class trap, the faster they can achieve their goals. Yes, a home is a necessity, and everybody gets into this trap for a time, but wise people get out of it as quickly as possible.

A home is a necessity, liability, and asset. I believe it is necessary that everybody owns a home where they and their families can live. I also believe it is important to purchase a home early enough that once you retire, your mortgage has been completely paid off. You don't want to pay rent or mortgage after you retire. You want to live the rest of your life free of stress, enjoying fruits of your labor.

A home is a huge expense. I can't stress enough how extremely important the largest purchase of your life is to your future financial health. So how can we pay off the debt of our primary home as soon as possible?

Here is one option that very few people consider: if and when you have the cash to pay off your debt, invest this money instead into other assets that pay you higher returns than the bank interest of your home loan. Obviously, you will need to invest these savings into other assets where your money can double more quickly. When you invest in other assets, your net worth will automatically increase.

Chapter 6

Escaping the Middle-Class Trap

L iving up to your means is so tempting, isn't it? When talking about this, a friend of mine was telling me about a sitcom he used to watch. In one episode, the main character and her friend are coaching another friend on how to shop. Their mantra was, "Spy, justify, and buy." In other words, you find something you like, justify why it is necessary for your happiness, then buy it. It was funny because it's relatable.

We see something we like, and our inner lawyer gets to work pleading against our better judgment. One of the most common arguments for buying liabilities is, "I can afford it, so why not?" We fall into this trap so easily, don't we? We feel the same when we buy a home. If I can afford it, why not buy the bigger, better house.

Once I had crunched the numbers and took an honest look at my net worth, my feeling of success vanished. I had a mortgage on both my car and home. My net worth was below zero, and nothing I was doing was getting me out of the trap. Fortunately for me, the down payment on the first condo I had bought during a buyer's market had not used up all my savings. I still had money left over for a down payment to invest in another.

It was a few years before I knuckled down and refocused on assets. When I did, I took out a second mortgage, bought another condo of the same size in the same building, and rented it out. Unfortunately, when I bought the second condo, prices had increased, and it was no longer a buyer's market. I had to buy at the normal market price. I wished I had buckled down and invested sooner, but it still made sense to buy at market price as it would give me a positive cash flow.

I should have bought two condos while it was a buyer's market, but fear kept me from buying another one. In the next chapter, we will see how fear can affect your decisions in your future and simple ways to overcome them.

I also approached the company I worked for with the hopes of making a deal where they would provide me with the car, and I would pay for the expenses. This would allow me to sell my own car, which, as we know, was a liability.

Since I was doing well and working hard, the company not only agreed to buy me a car but also agreed to pay the expenses. As if that weren't enough, they also upgraded me to a better car, further reducing my liabilities! Let me tell you, it never hurts to ask.

I did all this with the hope of moving from a negative net worth to a positive one. Any additional savings I have, I put into the new condo, and all this helped me speed up the doubling process.

Let's see what will happen to Stephen's net worth when he buys a big home for personal living versus what will happen if he buys a small home and an investment property. We will assume that property prices in Stephen's city are increasing at an annual rate of 3 percent, a rather modest growth.

U.S. census results conducted from 1968 to 2009 on the sale of new homes showed an average appreciation of 5.4 percent. The average appreciation in the last one hundred years has been around 3 percent. A quick search online will give you a clearer idea of long-term appreciation values in the area you are living in. For our example, we will stick with 3 percent.

The rule of 72 tells us that Stephen's home price will double every twenty-four years (72/3 = 24). Let's see how the doubling chart for Stephen's home will look like.

Doubling Chart For Stephen's $650,000 Home

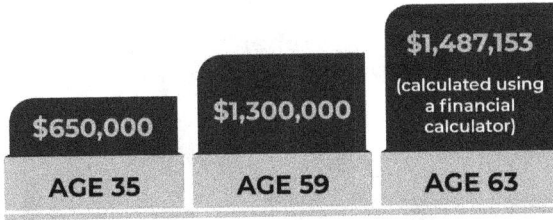

AGE 35	AGE 59	AGE 63
$650,000	$1,300,000	$1,487,153 (calculated using a financial calculator)

At sixty-three years old, Stephen's investment of $650,000 in his home has increased to $1,487,153. Although the value of Stephen's home has increased to $1,487,153, remember that this is his primary home, and we cannot take this into calculation of his real net worth.

Stephen's net worth at sixty-three is $0 (with no other assets or investments).

If Stephen chooses to downsize at sixty-three and sell his home to buy a smaller home at half the value $743,576.50, it would leave him with $743,576.50 in cash.

Stephen's net worth at sixty-three after downsizing is $743,576.50.

At the end of the chapter is a space to make this calculation for your own home. Take a little time to see what your net worth would be.

In this example, we are going to assume that Stephen, at thirty-five, bought his home for $650,000 in cash. We are making this a cash transaction purely to learn this concept. Later, when we study the concept of leverage, we will see what happens when Stephen has a home mortgage.

Now let's see what would happen if instead of buying a home for $650,000, Stephen decides to live in a smaller home at half the cost and use the other half of his money to buy an investment property from which he will receive rent every month. We will assume that the appreciation will be the same annually, at 3 percent. So the value of his home will double every twenty-four years. Look at his doubling chart with these changes!

Doubling Chart of Stephen's $325,000 Home (With 3 Percent Appreciation)

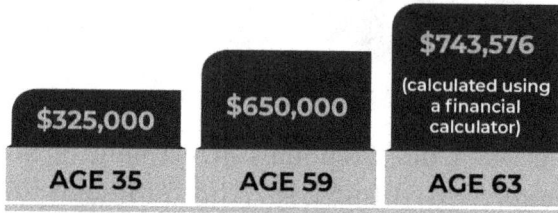

AGE 35	AGE 59	AGE 63
$325,000	$650,000	$743,576 (calculated using a financial calculator)

Stephen's investment property would have the exact same doubling chart, but it would also have a second doubling chart. The first doubling chart would show the same appreciation for his investment property as his primary home, and the other doubling chart would show the rental income received. (Stephen's $325,000 investment property will show an appreciated value of $743,576.)

For the sake of example, let's say that Stephen receives rental income of 10 percent per annum on his investment property. The rule of 72 tells us that he will double his money in seven years. The doubling chart for Stephen's rental income will look like this if he can successfully compound his rental income until retirement.

Doubling Chart of Stephen's Investment Property (Rental Income With 10 Percent Return)

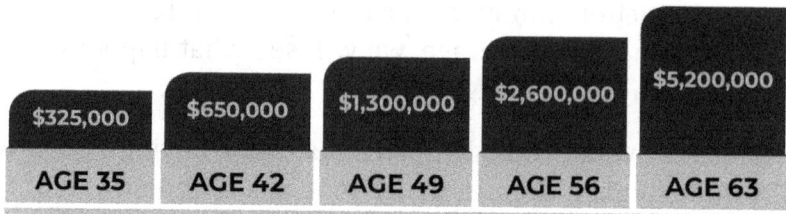

AGE 35	AGE 42	AGE 49	AGE 56	AGE 63
$325,000	$650,000	$1,300,000	$2,600,000	$5,200,000

So the value of his investment property plus new investment properties bought from rental income at sixty-three will be $743,576 + $5,200,000 = $5,943,576.

> To be able to compound his rental income, Stephen will have to buy more properties from the rental income he receives and rent them at annual return of 10 percent and keep doing so until the age of sixty-three. The figure at the age of sixty-three will be the value of all the investment properties he has bought from his rental income.

I don't want to complicate things by calculating the increase in value of all the investment properties Stephen will buy until the age of sixty-three. Suffice it to say, it will be a significant bonus.

By sixty-three, Stephen's primary home is worth $743,576, and his investment properties have a value of $5,943,576 that is a total of $6,687,152! We don't calculate the value of his primary home in his real net worth, but I would say he is still in pretty good shape.

The net worth of Stephen at the age of sixty-three is $5,943,576.

There is no comparison between a net worth of $5,943,576 and a net worth of $0 (or $743,576.50 after downsizing). Stephen was able to make an extra $5 million just by choosing to buy two homes at $325,000 rather than one home at $650,000.

The main choice here is between downsizing while you are young or downsizing after retirement. By making the decision to live a little more frugally and investing, he has increased and compounded his net worth to create an impressive nest egg and retire comfortably. Stephen has escaped the middle-class trap.

Keep in mind that this is just the concept. You know the right decisions for your life, but I hope, after seeing the difference this initial investment makes, you can learn to apply this concept to your own life in a way that works for you.

I know that when you have a family, you will need a bigger home as your children need space. I have a family of my own, but I can promise you that children often need less than our current culture tells us they need. They don't need a massive backyard to play football. Go take them to the playground or park to play.

I am not trying to say that buying one small home and another investment property is the only way to accumulate assets. A lot will depend on the financial climate and property cycle in your country. If property prices have peaked in your country, then you may find that splitting your money between a small home and certain stocks will be a better fit for you. You likely have the knowledge or can acquire the knowledge on how to invest in stocks to get better returns.

Maybe you can start a business where you can get higher returns on your money. The concept to learn here is that of splitting your money and then compounding and doubling it.

In this chapter, we assumed that the primary home and investment property were bought in cash so that we could better understand the concept. In the next chapter, we will get back to reality and see what happens when you borrow money to buy these properties.

Buying a home with a mortgage will put you in the middle-class trap, but the earlier you get into it, the earlier you can get out of it. You don't want to find yourself trapped in debt late in life. This will affect your financial future and leave you with less money to retire. Rent paid is money lost. It is money that could have been put into the process of doubling and compounding.

So let's recap.

Focus first on buying a home. Get into the middle-class trap early, and get out of it as soon as possible. At the same time, keep investing in assets that will put your money to work for you, doubling and compounding.

I know I keep nagging on about this, but I want to drive this point home—no matter where you are starting, if you apply the concepts from this book in your own life, you will achieve the financial security you desire.

Doubling Chart for My Home

At What Percentage Rate Does Your Home Increase In Value Every Year? (Check Online The Long-Term Average Property Appreciation Rates In Your Area.) Got That Number? It Is Likely To Be Around 3 To 5 Percent.

The Rule of 72 is 72 /... = ...Years.

$.................
(your home's
value today)

AGE ....

$.................
(this number
will be twice
that of the
current value)

AGE ....

$.................

AGE ....

$.................
By Retirement,
My Home Has
Increased
In Value To

AGE ....

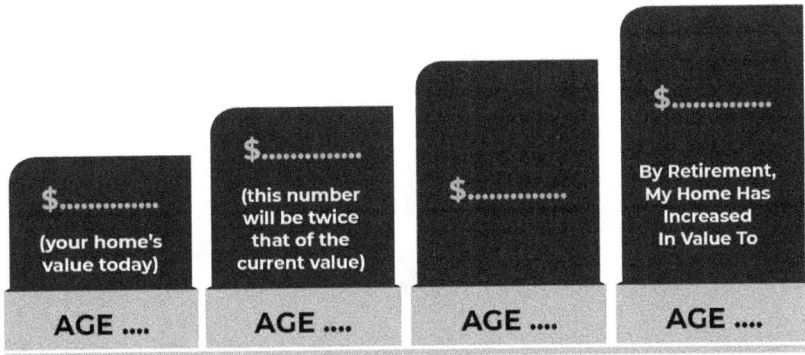

In the first blank, input your age and the present value of your home. In the second column, add the number of years and double the value of your home. Keep doing so until you reach the age of retirement.

Chapter 7

Leverage

Fear can immobilize us when we really should be moving. I could see that I needed to make some changes and that I needed to invest money to make money. That was a scary prospect. I had recently experienced how the Asian Financial Crisis had hit my adopted nation. I had witnessed the far-reaching effects on countries like South Korea and Japan, which had seemed like financial powerhouses but now were struggling.

How could I, just an average guy from India, ever think I could become a millionaire? My net worth was in the negative, so how was I supposed to invest? Borrowing was really my only option, but what if something happened and I couldn't pay it back?

I desperately longed to be able to talk to my dad. I needed some reassurance that I was moving in the right direction. I needed someone to come alongside me and encourage me to make bold but strategic choices.

To escape the middle-class trap, I had already determined I would need to buy an investment property when one became available in the building where I was living. I would be able to rent it out, and it was so close that managing it shouldn't be too big of a chore.

As I mentioned in the previous chapter, I still had enough savings for the down payment, but what bothered me was taking out that second mortgage. To borrow money from the bank when I still owed money on my primary residence felt like a heavy burden.

I didn't know if I was doing the right thing. My dad would have given me great advice, but he was gone. My mom was well versed in household management, but borrowing was never her domain.

To borrow or not to borrow, that was the question. I had to make a critical financial decision on my own, and I was petrified. Would this benefit or hinder my financial health? What if it turned out to be a bad choice? I had no one who could bail me out. The full responsibility was on my shoulders.

I again went to the books, doing my best to figure out if it really was worth the risk. It was during this time that I learned to apply the concept of leverage. When most of us hear the word *leverage*, we first think of what I call *mechanical leverage*. Think cantilevers, crowbars, and car jacks.

The types of leverage that we will explore in this chapter focus on ways to make you money: technological leverage, time leverage, and financial leverage. Before we get into all that, I want to paint a clear picture of mechanical leverage because I believe it is a good metaphor for all the others:

You and four friends have hit the open road in search of adventure. On a lonely highway, far from the lights of the city, one of your car tires suddenly bursts, and you come to a screeching halt. Luckily, you have an extra tire in your trunk, and you get it out to replace it.

You fish around in your trunk and realize that you don't have a jack. How on earth can you lift the car up to change the tire without a jack? So you look around, hoping to see lights of any passing cars, but all you see is the midnight blue of the empty asphalt for miles and miles in both directions. Your clever friends have already tried to call AMA, but there is no cell service.

Finally, the five of you decide that the strongest four should lift the car while the other one changes the tire. It is right around this point, as your arms shake with the strain and your vertebrae seem to be compacting more with each passing second, that you realize the importance of having a jack in the car.

It's true that 90 percent of the time, that jack is just taking up space in the trunk, but without a jack, lifting your car to change the tire is almost impossible. With a jack, four of you could hang out whistling show tunes while the other got the job done. Instead, you need five people working hard just to change your flat tire.

This is leverage at its most basic.

Technological Leverage

Let me tell you the story of Oliver.

He works every night as a singer at a restaurant in Atlanta. He is really good. All the patrons love him, and his bosses are always pleased with his performance. Oliver's problem is that he only gets paid on the days he sings. If he gets sick or when something comes up to keep him from working, he is out of pocket for that day. If Oliver gets a friend to sing on his behalf, it's his friend that gets paid; after all, he's the one that earned it.

I call jobs like this "do-it-yourself" (or DIY) work. The kinds of jobs where you get paid only when you do it yourself are not usually jobs where you make a lot of money. They have no leverage. The only way Oliver can really advance this career is by using technology. If he records his music, he can reach a wider audience, and his music can be sold at any time of the day. In this instance, the online music and CDs are doing Oliver's job for him.

This is technological leverage.

The Internet can be used as technological leverage in many ways. For example, *Amazon* doesn't need salespeople to attend their clients or even need a store, as people from all over the world go to their website and buy stuff. *Amazon* saves money on salaries of salespeople and on the rental of physical stores.

Perhaps there is some technology you can leverage to make you money. Maybe you can be the next *YouTube* star. Maybe you have amazing musical ability and can put out an online album. Maybe you can start your own online business or write a book. Ask yourself if there is a way that technology can do the hard work for you.

Time Leverage

We all have an equal amount of time in a day. We each get twenty-four hours to work, eat, sleep, and enjoy life. How can we get more accomplished than we have the time for? How do we leverage time?

A music lover, Frank is the owner of that restaurant in Atlanta. He figures that if he has a live music act, he will attract more customers and increase business. Frank is both the owner and head chef. Although he himself is a talented performer, he can't leave the kitchen long enough to perform.

So he needs the time and skill of someone else to bring in the customers. This is time leverage. All businesses use employees to run successfully. If you are a company employee, that company is leveraging your time and skill to make money.

In the previous example, we saw that Oliver is a singer—it's a DIY work. If he is not on the job, he cannot get paid. There are loads of jobs where it is impossible to leverage time. A surgeon doesn't get paid if he does not operate. A writer doesn't get paid if they don't write, and teachers don't get paid if they don't teach.

Leveraging other people's time allows you to put your own time to its optimum use.

If you are in a job where you can't leverage time, it is time to ask yourself if there is any other type of leverage you can use to get ahead in life. It's time to look at the most common and useful leverage of all.

Financial Leverage

This is the only real leverage a worker can have. We need financial leverage, or we will be left behind, unable to buy any assets.

Financial leverage is when we use other people's money to buy an asset or run a business. Although it is the easiest leverage to use for financial gain, it is also the riskiest.

Buying a rental property or running a business with money borrowed from the bank is financial leverage. There are groups of people who will find that this is still a difficult thing to leverage. People who work freelance or run small businesses most commonly struggle to leverage money. When you are freelancing or running a small business, it is harder to show actual income. Also, to minimize taxation, you need to show higher expenses in the company and therefore resulting in little or no profit. This does not look good on paper when you are applying for a bank loan.

Stephen does not have a business of his own but does have a decent job. Therefore he has a better chance of using financial leverage. The salary of someone employed in full-time work looks steadier and less risky than someone who has a small business of their own but not a steady paycheck.

The banks love to lend money to guys like Stephen. So even though Stephen cannot leverage time, he can leverage money. His steady job and a good income become an asset in this case.

Let's see how Stephen uses financial leverage. In the previous chapter, "Escaping the Middle-Class Trap," we saw what happens to Stephen's financial future when he buys a home for $650,000 and what happens when he splits his money to buy two properties at $325,000 each. Stephen had saved a whopping $65,000, which is an incredible amount, but not enough to buy the houses outright. So he needed to take out a mortgage from the bank.

Let's assume that due to taxes (which vary in every country), agent fees, and other maintenance expenses, the return on Stephen's investment property was only 8 percent: 10 percent was the gross return before taxes and expenses, and 8 percent is the net return after taxes and expenses.

Let's see how Stephen's doubling chart will look with the net 8 percent return. According to the rule of 72, he will double his money every nine years (72/8 = 9).

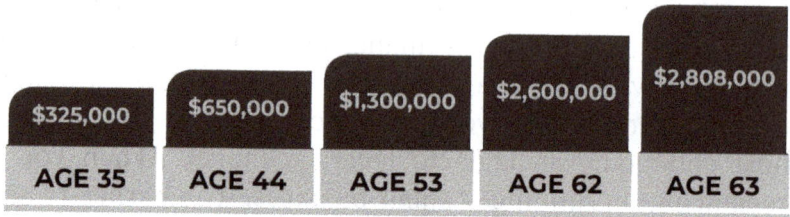

$325,000	$650,000	$1,300,000	$2,600,000	$2,808,000
AGE 35	AGE 44	AGE 53	AGE 62	AGE 63

You can see that with just a 2 percent drop in return, the value of Stephen's investment was almost halved. The value of his investment at age sixty-three at 8 percent return is $2,808,000, but the value of investment at age sixty-three at 10 percent return was $5,200,000. This is what a 2 percent drop can do to your money in the long term. The net worth of Stephen at sixty-three after taxes and expenses is $3,551,576.

> **If Stephen desires the same net worth as above examples at sixty-three, he needs to pay the bank mortgage for his primary home and his investment property from his own earnings. The rent received from the investment property must be reinvested to acquire new investments properties that will give him an 8 percent net return or higher.**

For people like Stephen, who start with nothing and have no capital, this is a good way to build it. By choosing to pay the mortgage of his first investment property from his active income, Stephen could maintain the same volume of money he wanted to put into the process of doubling, which is $325,000, the value of his investment property.

If Stephen can pay a mortgage for the $650,000 home from his earnings, it stands to reason that he will be able to pay a mortgage for two properties at $325,000 from his earnings too. This is crucial. If Stephen doesn't pay the mortgage of both properties from his own earnings, he won't be able to use the rental income from investment property to invest further and achieve the $3,551,576 net worth that we see in our doubling charts.

The mortgage rate for the $650,000 home over twenty-eight years at a rate of 4 percent, with a 10 percent down payment, will be $2,896 per month. Let's make the reasonable assumption that by the time Stephen is thirty-five, his income has gone up, and he can afford this mortgage.

If you buy two properties at $325,000 each and put down the same down payment and borrow the remainder for twenty-eight years at a rate of 4 percent, the monthly mortgage will be the exact same amount.

Remember! As much as it may hurt some months, you must pay the mortgage for your first investment property from your own earnings and not from your rental income. Rental income should be saved in another separate account while you wait for the right opportunity to buy your next investment property. This is extremely important. So important, in fact, that I encourage you to make this pledge to yourself!

Say it out loud, and it will feel more like you mean it:

> **"I will not spend my rental income or profits from my investments buying clothes, purses, watches, cars, or vacations. I will not even use it on my children's education. My rental income or profits from my investments are to be solely used for reinvestment."**

There, didn't that feel good? Now, remember to stick to it. It's the only way this is really going to work for you. This is the most important part of the concept if you want to be successful. After you buy your second investment property, you can use your rental income from the first and second investment property to pay the mortgage of the second investment property. With two incomes working to pay off your third mortgage, it will cut in half the time it would take to finish paying it off.

Top Tip

Working couples who want to invest in this way will maximize their profits if they each purchase these properties under their own names. This way, both can get personal income tax deductions or benefits, depending on the country in which you live.

Additionally, you can start a small company for your real estate dealings and buy in your company's name with the aim of minimizing taxes.

To maximize profits and minimize taxes, some homework will be required to find which avenue will prove most beneficial.

By doing this, Stephen's net worth at sixty-three would be $3,551,576.

You may be saying to yourself, "Wait a minute! I was nervous when you said get two mortgages, but three? No way!"

I totally understand if it's out of your comfort zone. I was more than a little anxious myself when I took out that third mortgage. I wasn't some rich kid with a parental safety net to fall back on, and I like to sleep well at night. My mental and physical health are as important as my financial health. I always leveraged what I could afford and never overdid it.

Also, what helped me was the timing. I was investing at a time when the property prices had collapsed and were just recovering. If property prices are at an all-time high, it won't be wise to take on multiple mortgages.

Remember, investments like this are meant for our future financial security, not to show off or compete. You will make good financial decisions when your intentions are to leverage for your future financial security.

If it is out of your comfort zone to take on a third mortgage, then you can choose to pay off the mortgage of your first investment property first. Once you have no mortgage on the first investment property, you can use the rental income from this property to buy a second investment property. Your net worth will appear much lower if you do this because you won't be doubling money as per our doubling charts, but it will still be better than if you failed to reinvest that rental income at all.

The fear I had when I had to take out the second mortgage quickly dissipated. My choice of buying two small properties instead of one big one for my personal home meant I was still living within my means. Since I could afford to pay the mortgage on a big home, I could afford to pay mortgage on two smaller ones. Even if I couldn't find a tenant, I wasn't worried. I knew I could afford to pay both mortgages anyway.

As you can see, splitting your money to invest in a primary home and a rental property, as mentioned above, is a great choice. It will not only take you out of the middle-class trap but also make you a millionaire by retirement. Of course, this doesn't happen overnight. In the beginning, growth is slow, and it may feel like you aren't getting anywhere. That's why the vision and the vow are so important.

Waiting for bamboo to grow is a lot like waiting for your investments to mature. In the first two years after planting, bamboo is busy getting rooted. You may see one or two shoots break ground, but it is an unimpressive showing. It isn't until its third year that bamboo suddenly shoots up in culms. As soon as it peeks out of the ground, the bamboo is already at the diameter it will continue to be for its lifespan. In the right conditions, it can grow up to three feet a day.

Investments in properties are like that. Your investment upfront is large, and you may wonder if it was worthwhile, but hang in there. After a time, as your investment matures, you will see what appears to be sudden and abundant growth.

What I haven't included in our calculations—but is really the icing on the cake—is that all the investment properties that Stephen will buy until his retirement appreciates over time, and his net worth will skyrocket.

Also, all this is a result of a onetime investment at the age of thirty-five! If Stephen manages to find low-cost/high-return properties and has money left over to invest further, his net worth at sixty-three may even be much higher than we have predicted here.

The key to using leverage successfully is common sense, realistic assumptions, and a clear understanding of the risks. Leverage can make you very rich. But, as I mentioned at the beginning of the chapter, there are real risks involved. So do your homework.

The Beauty of Financial Leverage

The first year rental return on Stephen's $325,000 rental x 8%	= $26,000
The first year 4 percent cost of interest on $292,500 will be	= $11,700
Net profit for the first year	= $14,300

Can you believe it? On an investment of $32,500, Stephen makes a profit of $14,300[2]. So his cash on cash return is at 44 percent. Some people find it impossible to get a 10 percent return on their investments while others easily get a return of 44%.

We also assume that appreciation in the value of his investment property will be 3 percent. So after the first year, the increase in value of his property will be $9,750[3], which is an additional 30 percent return.

The total return in the 1st year on the $32,500 cash invested by Stephen would be 74 percent.

---

[2] A 44 percent return in the first year
[3] That is another 30% percent additional return on the cash $32,500 invested by Stephen

The real beauty of using leverage comes when you employ two or more types of leverages at the same time. Successful businesses make a lot of money because they implement all types of leverages simultaneously. They have employees, so they can leverage their time and skill. They leverage both technology and money.

If your goal is to "make it big," owning a business where you can leverage time, technology, and money is the way to go. But let's face it. We can't all be Warren Buffett or Richard Branson. Many of us wouldn't want to be.

Chapter 8

Good Debt, Bad Debt, And Positive Cash Flow

Have you ever seen the movie *The Joneses*, starring Demi Moore and David Duchovny?

The movie tells the story of an average, upper-middle-class family that moves into an average, upscale suburban area, showing off their perfect family and their perfect life. What folks in the neighborhood don't realize is that the Joneses are, in fact, all actors, hired to sell products to their neighbors. Their strategy is to live life in a way that makes those around them take notice.

When Mr. Jones buys his wife a gift for her birthday, he asks the advice of his friends, all the while subtly swaying them to believe that to have a great life and a perfect marriage, they need to buy a specific brand of jewelry or clothing. When he plays golf, he refuses certain brands of clubs, in favor of others, implying that the brand he uses is far superior and will help anyone's game.

When the Jones kids go to school in their brand-name clothes and speak with enthusiasm about the game systems, trips, or the latest trends from New York and Paris they want to take, other kids naturally want to keep up. The movie accurately portrays our need to compete with those around us. People are willing to get into debt to stay a part of the in-crowd. It reminds me of an old Indian expression, "The teeth the elephant shows the world are different from the teeth he actually eats with."

As soon as my daughter is old enough to understand, I will warn her to watch out for guys with flashy cars, but not just because they could be dirtbags. I hope that I can give her a good, solid financial education that will help her learn to watch for the character of a person rather than their outward impression. In my experience, the "really rich" don't feel the need to show off in the same way the "feeling rich" do.

There are very few people that willfully shun debt. I personally know only a handful, but I think most of us might know at least one. My friend's dad is like this. He is the kind of guy that doesn't believe in having a debt of any sort. Whatever he buys, he buys in cash—be it food, clothing, vacation, or even property. Although this is a less common practice in the west, many Asians choose to live in this way. Many believe this is the only way to have a debt-free, stress-free lifestyle.

"Cash only" sounds good in theory, but in truth, only a small percentage of the population has enough resources to buy all that they need in cash, especially when it comes to owning a home or starting a business. The average person needs to borrow money to afford more costly items. Don't get me wrong. I am not advocating debt for its own sake, but not all debt is bad debt, and one must know the difference.

It is still important to keep this in mind: the poor borrow money to buy necessities, the middle class borrow money to buy liabilities, and the rich borrow money to buy assets. No matter where you have started, there is always a way to climb out of poverty.

> **Money borrowed to buy necessities and liabilities is bad debt.**
>
> **Money borrowed to buy assets is good debt!**

We have looked at the case of Thomas, who buys a car as soon as he gets a job, borrowing money in order to buy it. This is the fastest way to shrink your money by half. It is what I would call a middle-class focus. Borrowing money on items that will lose value is bad debt.

Borrowing money for a vacation is most definitely bad debt. Going shopping for brand-name clothes, perfumes, purses, or any other liabilities on credit is also very bad debt. If you intend to buy liabilities like this, it is important to save and use cash so that you will limit the liability it will have on your net income.

I have also developed a habit of asking salespeople if they would offer a discount on larger items if I pay cash. If they offer even a 3 or 5 percent discount on cash, it is worth it to use cash. However, if there is no cash discount, then I would choose to pay by credit card to get points.

Credit card points can often be converted into airline miles, gas cards, hotel room rentals, and even cash. I try to do my homework and choose a credit card that gives the highest points for money spent and often get free vacations.

The "rich" mindset focuses on doubling money. As we saw in the last chapter, Stephen borrowed money to buy an income property and doubled his money many times over, and by retirement had a multimillion-dollar nest egg.

Basically, any money borrowed to increase your income is good debt. This includes money borrowed for your education, as this should increase your income in the future. Money borrowed to start a business is good debt if it leads to profits that increase your income.

Money borrowed to buy a positive-cash-flowing asset is good debt.

Money borrowed to buy a negative-cash-flowing asset is bad debt.

I suppose you might like some specific examples of the two. So let's take a closer look at a positive-cash-flowing asset and a negative-cash-flowing asset.

We'll look again at the example of Steven's investments to study what a positive-cash-flowing asset and negative-cash-flowing asset are. We saw how Steven invested his $65,000 on a down payment to buy a home and investment property. He had to borrow 90 percent of the remainder from the bank to buy both these properties. We saw that he bought two properties with a value of $325,000 each and split his down payment between both, putting down $32,500 on each.

He borrowed money from the bank at an interest rate of 4 percent for twenty-eight years.

Stephen's Investment Property

Property Value	$325,000
Down Payment	$32,500
Principle	$292,500
Interest	4%
Year	28

This meant that he would pay a monthly installment of $1,448 (calculated by a financial calculator).

Stephen rented his investment property and got a rental return of 8 percent on the value of the property after taxes and expenses. So the annual rental income that Stephen receives will be $26,000[4]. If you divide this amount by twelve months, it will give you $2,166, the monthly rental income that Steven receives each month.

To recap, Steven pays a monthly installment of $1,448 to the bank but receives $2,166 from his tenant. This means that Steven can easily pay $1,448 to the bank every month and be left over with $718.

This extra money is called a *positive cash flow*.

---

[4] $325,000 x 8% = $26,000

What would happen if Stephen was only able to get an annual rental return of 5 percent? What would happen to his cash flow?

Now the rental return Steven will receive will be $325,000 x 5 percent = $16,250 per annum. His monthly rent would be $1,354, which is less than the $1,448 that he has to pay the bank. So, in this case, the rent received is not enough to pay the bank, and Steven will be paying $94 to the bank from his own pocket.

This is called *negative cash flow*.

This calculation works the same way with his primary home. He will pay his monthly installment of $1,448 to the bank, but as he lives in his home, there will be no income from it. Every month he must pay the bank $1,448 from his own pocket. This is a negative cash flow and a liability as it is taking money out of his pocket. The upside is that he saves on rent, and in the end, he will have an asset.

Even though the value of his primary home will appreciate with time, it's still considered bad debt since we never calculate the value of a primary home into your net worth. Even if the primary home triples or quadruples in value over time, it's of no use as Stephen still needs a home to live, and the appreciated value of his primary home won't add to his net worth.

People who buy assets only for appreciation will not see much growth. Buying one or two properties in hope of appreciation only will mean that for a very long time, you will experience a negative cash flow. You won't be able to buy more properties as there is a limit to the loss you can bear. It's like continuing to run a business at a loss.

Let's say you open a coffee shop, and people love it. You have the clientele. You have what appears to be a thriving business, and people suggest you open more of these awesome coffeehouses all over the city. The problem is that you are not making a profit. You aren't even breaking even. There is no way you can start a new coffee shop when your current one is making a loss. This is the same as having a negative-cash-flow property.

But when you buy positive-cash-flow properties, there is no limit to the number of properties you can buy. Each subsequent property pays for the next. You could buy five, ten—even a hundred properties. You will have a lot more paperwork and more to manage, but you will also have a larger and larger positive cash flow.

Most of my friends who bought properties only for their appreciation subsequently received a negative cash flow and stopped buying more properties, especially when the market went down.

If you have a positive cash flow, appreciation is guaranteed. Appreciation is a by-product of a positive cash flow. Of course, appreciation depends on supply and demand and various other factors, but we are going to focus on having a positive cash flow as many people don't know its importance.

I learned a lot from my experience of buying my first investment property. A new world of investing in properties opened to me, which would eventually make me a millionaire and financially secure. The decision to buy a small home and invest the other half into an investment property changed my entire life. It triggered a streak of property buying, which has slowly and steadily lead me toward financial success.

The difference between the multibillionaire Warren Buffett's home and Michael Jackson's Neverland Ranch tells this story. Warren Buffett could afford to live in several large palaces, but compared to his net worth, his home is rather conservative. Michael Jackson's home and lifestyle became a money pit, which placed him in a precarious financial position several times.

The reason movies like *The Joneses* hit a nerve is that we are all susceptible to the lure of money. We all wonder what it would be like to live the lifestyle of the rich and famous. National lotteries exist because people hope and dream of being pulled out of their ordinary life—dreams of having money that could change the course of their life forever.

For many, the desire of this lifestyle is the very thing that compels them to purchase luxury items that will only incur really bad debt.

The latest edition of Credit Suisse's Global Wealth Report in mid-2019 shows that there are about 46.8 million (USD) millionaires globally. Considering the global population in 2019 is about 7.7 billion people, the total number of millionaires comprises almost 0.61 percent of the world's population.

Now, let's see if we can add your name to that list!

Chapter 9

Active and Passive Income (Work for Your Money, and Let Your Money Work for You)

Many of us understand the importance of bringing home a regular paycheck. It's a lesson we first learn from our parents, who want to raise children with good careers and an active income. In Indian culture, there is no "following your dreams." We become teachers, doctors, marketing professionals, accountants, or engineers. Sports and arts are only encouraged if you actually have the talent to achieve stardom.

There is another type of income that most eastern parents would never think to encourage their children to pursue: passive income. No one talks about it. Very few even know the term. We are a culture where hard work is glorified, and "taking the easy way" is for lazy sluggards, who won't amount to much.

My parents were just the same as other Indian parents. They believed it was their duty to lecture and push me to attain high grades. If I failed to do that, I was in for a spanking. I'm not speaking figuratively. In addition to school, my dad would tutor me and check my homework. Even in those tutoring sessions, he would sometimes give me a good swat if I got an answer wrong.

I'm not telling you this so that you get mad at my dad and think I was living with all sorts of abuse. I loved my dad, and I know that he had the best intentions. My dad just wanted me to do well in school. If I didn't, he worried that I would suffer for it as an adult. At least, I know that now. As a kid, I admit, I didn't really get it. I just wanted to play with my friends, watch TV, and forget studying.

One day, after a well-deserved spanking, I got so angry that I decided to run away from home. I was probably about fifteen or sixteen at the time. It's a fun age, isn't it? With righteous anger bubbling up from a well of teenage angst, I decided I didn't need to take it anymore. I would run away from home.

I thought I was so clever as I pulled one T-shirt over another, over another, and over another until I had four or five shirts on and could barely move my arms at the shoulder. I pulled on some shorts and put on a pair of jeans, ran out the front door, grabbed my bike, and started pedaling. I was so angry that I got pretty far, pretty fast. After a couple of hours, I was already outside of the city.

By then, my anger had subsided a little. I thought of my mother and my sister. I would miss them. They would probably cry and think it was their fault. I wouldn't be around to assure them it had nothing to do with them.

Another hour passed, and I realized I didn't want to leave them behind. I could endure. I could press on, for them. Noble, don't you think?

Looking back, I am actually grateful to my dad for trying to discipline me and teach me the importance of having a good income. Now that I am an adult, I can see how my active income has helped me be able to build a passive income. In fact, I often wish I had studied harder and listened to him when it came to my education.

Thinking back, during his life, my dad taught me the importance of active income, and in his death, he taught me the importance of having a passive income. Dad was a doctor. It's a DIY job, so when he got sick, there was no way for him to leverage time. Since he couldn't leverage time and didn't have enough invested to build a passive income for himself, he was in a spot of financial trouble that affected the whole family.

My father's illness and eventual death was the hard lesson I needed to discipline myself to save and invest for passive income.

Active income is your most important income. It is your base. The bigger the base, the better. A teacher earning a salary of $45,000 a year won't have the same investment budget as a doctor earning $100,000 a year. A doctor is unlikely to have the same investment budget as an A-list celebrity, who earns millions per picture. Active income is a direct result of your ability, capability, and time spent working in your respective fields.

Passive income, as we mentioned earlier, is income you receive

> **Note: When I decided to pay the mortgage of my primary home and investment property from my active income, it made me a millionaire.**

without putting too much of your own time into earning it. A few hours of maintenance a month, a few big decisions here and there, and your investment earns money for you. If you are sick, you are still earning money. If you're away on holiday, you are still earning money. You can sit in your living room binge-watching *Netflix*, and you will still be earning money.

Our lives tend to revolve around our work. We focus so hard on achieving the highest level of active income that we never pay much attention to passive income, which is commonly earned from investments.

Although we haven't labeled them as such, in previous chapters, we've already looked at several examples of passive income. Dividends from stocks, rental income, interest on savings, or fixed deposits—all these things fall under the category of passive income.

Some passive incomes don't require an active income. People with certain talents can earn royalties on sales of their CDs, books, patents, or movies long after they have released them.

Occasionally, the royalties will be enough that it will provide all they need for a secure retirement. But very few of us are the next J. K. Rowling or Simon Cowell, whose passive incomes are so high they could retire and live like royalty.

Think of active income and passive income like your own two legs. You need both (or a good prosthetic) to run. If one of your legs were to become suddenly useless, you would limp and struggle to do what you could have done easily before. Even if you were born missing a limb, you would still spend a good deal of your life finding ways to compensate for something you have never had.

In the same way, if you have only one type of income, you will neither be able to do what those with both types of income can do nor have the same type of security. You need both incomes, active and passive, to be able to run financially. Despite this, most people rely on only one type of income, usually their career-related active income, with which they run their entire life. As a result, they often struggle financially.

Many people, who do not earn enough to cover their monthly budget, take on a second job. This is all well and good, but this is still only increasing your active income. What you need to work out is your other "leg." You need to start letting the money you have earned work for you. The aim is not to have more active jobs. When you try and juggle multiple jobs, you will eventually burn out.

Your real aim should be to increase your passive income. Once your passive income is big enough to support your lifestyle, you could even choose to retire. This is where those multiple investments come into play. We've seen in the example of Stephen that for his first investment property to make him a millionaire, he must pay the mortgage of this investment property from his earnings or active income.

This is where you see both "legs" working together to make him a millionaire—with active and passive each becoming the other's security. If Stephen were to lose his renter for a time, he doesn't need to worry about losing his property because the mortgage payment is not reliant on the rental income. To really exercise the passive income leg, Stephen needs to be willing to take on multiple investments.

Like I pointed out in the previous chapters, Stephen only has to pay for his first investment property from his active income. The mortgage on the second investment property and all future properties he buys can be paid from the rental income received from any of his properties.

Once both legs are working together, he will see rapid growth in his net worth. If he has extra money saved from his active income, he can use this money to pay off one of his investment properties in cash, increasing his positive cash flow and eventually his net worth.

The beauty of passive income is that it's "easy money." After you sign the papers and find a renter, there is very little else for you to do. Apart from occasional repairs when required, money will come in each month (make sure you vet your renters properly, as you don't want renters known for skipping payments), and your main job will be depositing it in the bank and deciding how to reinvest.

At this point, you may see dollar signs floating in front of your eyes, feeling like Scrooge McDuck swimming in a pool of gold coins. If that's the case, give yourself a slap and get yourself grounded. This isn't like winning the lottery.

Passive income is easy money, but to keep that passive income coming, you will need to be paying the mortgages from your active income and sticking to the budget for your living expenses. You will still need to clock in at work each day. If you don't, you may as well kiss that passive income goodbye; it will do nothing to secure your future.

Once you have done this a few times, and managing properties starts to turn into real work, it's a good idea to hire a property manager. Yes, you will have to dip into some of the rental income, but it will allow you to continue with a strong flow of passive income. A healthy passive income will mean more time for your family. More time for yourself. More time to exercise. More money to eat healthy. It means early retirement and lengthy vacations.

Our active income is the path to a steady and long-term passive income.

Chapter 10

Four-Dimensional Investing

A long, long time ago, back before many of us can even re-member— before the internet, before fax machines, be-fore cassette tapes and eight-track tapes—there was a technology so groundbreaking people believed it to be magic. They called it "moving pictures." Black and white, grainy, sound-less, it had the ability to inspire awe.

People were happy and content seeing moving pictures on their screen. They had no idea that, in a short time, the technology would advance drastically. For the sake of teaching the concepts in this chapter, I am going to call these original moving pictures, "one-dimensional movies."

By 1927, the world was introduced to the first "talkie." Suddenly, people could hear what their favorite stars sounded like. With the addition of dialogue and music, moving pictures took on another dimension. So we will call motion pictures with sound, "two-dimensional movies."

Again, it seemed like magic. This second dimension added a dash of realism that wasn't there before. When the movie *King Kong* came out, people were so convinced it was real that there were reports of people having heart attacks in the theater.

The 1950s brought us the "golden age of cinema." Moving pictures now had glorious Technicolor and improved sound quality, and movie houses across America began to show films in 3D. A little pair of blue-and-red glasses had the ability to make you feel as if you were right there in the action. What could possibly be better than this? People really believed they were living at the pinnacle of motion-picture technology. These "three-dimensional movies" were as real as real could be. This was a form of movie magic that could never be topped.

Except it was. I had my first experience of four-dimensional movies at Universal Studios in Los Angeles a little while back, and it was incredible! My seat moved along with the action of the film. The sound surrounded me, so that if someone was speaking from off the screen, it felt like they were right behind me. One of the characters jumped into a pool, and water splashed on us. It was a gift to the senses, and for the duration of the film, I was living in another world.

We all left that theatre with an expression of wonder on our faces. This four-dimensional movie was the ultimate experience. This is the same experience we want to have with our investments. It is one thing to invest in something that will appreciate, but it is another thing for those investments to develop to a place where the investments are not only working for you (passive income) but are also creating opportunities to leverage and free up your time for other pursuits.

The Four Dimensions of An Investment

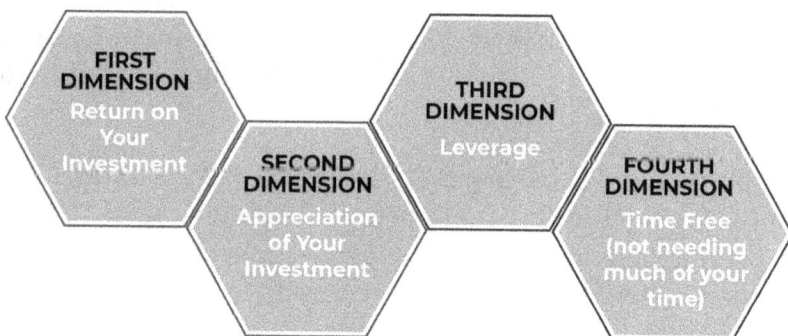

FIRST DIMENSION
Return on Your Investment

SECOND DIMENSION
Appreciation of Your Investment

THIRD DIMENSION
Leverage

FOURTH DIMENSION
Time Free (not needing much of your time)

One-Dimensional Investment

With one-dimensional investing, you receive back on only one of the above four dimensions on your investment. When I think of one-dimensional investing, day trading springs to mind. With day trading, you receive only the appreciation on your investment. You do not receive a return or dividend.

Day trading requires that you put your time in doing it every day. If you could leverage money, it would become a two-dimensional investment, but it's high risk. No leverage means no second dimension. The only dimension of the investment is appreciation.

Two-Dimensional Investment

Two-dimensional investment adds a secondary dimension to your investment. If you were to buy a couple of gold bars and keep them in your safety box, you will see that investment appreciate over time.

There is little else for you to do but sit and wait for that appreciation to happen. It's not something you will need to work at—it's time free. However, there is no return on this investment, and there is nothing you can leverage. So, in this case, you will receive reparations from the two dimensions of your investment: appreciation and being time free.

Savings and fixed bank accounts are other examples of two-dimensional investments. You deposit money in the bank and then let it sit. Over time, you will get a return or interest on your investment. You don't have to do anything to achieve it. Again, it is time free. However, there is nothing to leverage here, and you will not find that the money has appreciated.

In fact, because of inflation, if Stephen were to place $32,500 in a savings account today instead of using it as a down payment on a property. The likelihood that thirty years from now that $32,500 will allow him to place a down payment on a property of equivalent size is very low. So you will receive payment on only two dimensions on this investment: a return and being time free.

Short-term investment in the stock market would also fall under the category of two-dimensional investing. Short-term investment in stocks will provide you with a return in the form of a dividend. You can receive appreciation on the value of your stocks, but it means that you will have to monitor it all the time. It's not "time free," and there is nothing for you to leverage. In the absence of leverage, this investment will give you reparations on two dimensions: return and appreciation.

You may notice that I haven't paid much attention to the second dimension of appreciation. I've noticed that the mindset of the general population is focused on this second dimension. Buy low, pray for appreciation, then sell to get a profit. I want to change this mindset.

If the moviemakers stopped all technological advances after the invention of the talkie, our future would have been very different. There would be no smartphones with video calling. There would be no live news broadcasts.

So don't just settle for appreciation when you can have so much more. I don't give much importance to appreciation in real estate investing. Appreciation doesn't give us any cash flow, and you only benefit from it if you sell the investment.

Similarly, you may think your property has tripled in value, but it has not actually tripled in value until you find a buyer willing to pay you triple your investment. Many property investors never plan to sell their properties. They like to hold them forever and pass them on to the next generation. If you never plan on selling, it doesn't matter if it has appreciated three times or six times. To enjoy the benefits, one needs to add another dimension to their investments: a healthy return.

Three-Dimensional Investment

Long-term investments in the stock market are probably the best example of three-dimensional investing. You will receive a return or dividend on your investment. You receive appreciation on its value over time, and it's relatively time free. Because you don't plan to sell any time soon, there is no reason to monitor it daily. You make a one-time, well-informed decision to invest and then don't have to look at it maybe for a couple of years or more.

When I tell my friends that buying stocks is three-dimensional investing, they are quick to disagree. They insist that you can also use leverage in the stock market. But when I ask them if they use leverage, the answer is often no. Without leverage, it is still just three-dimensional. Leveraging stocks is high-risk and requires a higher level of intelligence to do it, and most people don't qualify.

Let's look at what happens when you don't leverage or cannot use leverage in the stock purchasing. We'll go back to the example of Stephen. Stephen had saved $65,000 to invest. He split that amount between two down payments: $32,500 for his primary home, $32,500 for an investment property.

This time, instead of investing $32,500 as down payment for the investment property, he invests this money in the stock market. Let's assume that Stephen neither has an appetite for risk nor the intelligence required to use leverage in the stock market. However, Stephen is intelligent enough to get 10 percent returns on his money constantly every year.

According to the rule of 72, he will double his money every seven years, and his doubling chart for his investment in stock market will look like this:

**Doubling Chart of Stephen's Stock Investment
(Annual Rate of 10 Percent)**

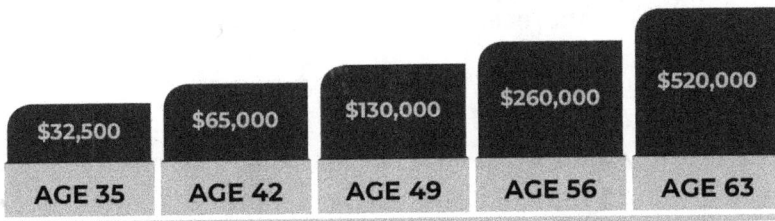

AGE 35	AGE 42	AGE 49	AGE 56	AGE 63
$32,500	$65,000	$130,000	$260,000	$520,000

If you compare this to his investment in the rental property, it's a huge difference in net profit. If you remember, Stephen's $325,000 investment property gave him $2,808,000 when invested at a rate of 8 percent after taxes. Why is there such a huge difference between the two investments, $520,000 by the age of 63 investing in stocks and $2.8 million by the age of 63 investing in a rental property?

There are two reasons for this to happen. First is the loss of one of the dimensions—leverage. Without leverage, Stephen gets a 10 percent return on the $32,500 invested in the stock market, but with leverage, Stephen gets an 8 percent return on $325,000, which is the value of the investment property. So the volume of money put into the process of doubling is the problem.

A second important factor to remember is that Stephen could only double the entire value of his $325,000 investment because he was paying the mortgage on this investment property from his active income. Since Stephen committed to paying the mortgage from his active income, it means that every month, he is contributing to his savings. He can't just spend this money on whatever he feels like; this money is locked into receiving a return of 8 percent every year until the time the mortgage is over.

Now, if Stephen were to choose to invest $32,500 in stocks instead, he will have no mortgage to pay, and that money would be available to him every month. If Stephen would religiously invest this same amount of money as the mortgage payment in stocks every year and get a 10 percent return on this money, then this amount could be very big by the age of 63. It could even surpass the amount received by investing in the rental property.

But what happens when you have extra money every month? Usually, we are tempted to spend it on vacations or other liabilities. It would be very hard for you to be as disciplined investing a fixed amount in stocks every month. Finding the right stocks to invest in every month is not easy to do. The amount of time required to do this means that you will not be able to access that fourth dimension: "time-free income."

When you pay the mortgage from your active income, two important forces come into play:

The first one is monthly investing. It will automatically force you to invest every month in your investment property. To be able to do it, it will force you to live frugally instead of frivolously. You will cut your expenses. You will learn to discipline yourself and your spending habits.

Secondly, reinvesting. Your rental income will keep accumulating monthly in your account. To compound this money, you will be forced to reinvest it to receive an 8 percent return. To do so, your focus will shift from other unimportant things in your life to finding properties that give you an 8 percent return. When you have the right focus, your actions will follow to find such properties, and your chance of success will be higher.

Investment in your business also fits under the category of three-dimensional investing. You can receive returns or profits from your company, the value of your company can go up, and you also can use leverage by borrowing money from the bank or by finding investors to start or stimulate your business. But since you will have to manage it by yourself and will need your time and energy to make it successful, it's only going to be a three-dimensional investment.

Four-Dimensional Investing

We saw how Stephen invested in a rental property getting an 8 percent return—this was his first dimension. This property will appreciate over time with an average annual appreciation of 3 percent—his second dimension.

By using the third dimension, leverage, Stephen could purchase a property of greater value than he could afford. Once that investment is made, and renters are in place, there is little time investment needed from Stephen, and this freeing up of his time finally adds that fourth dimension that will ultimately make Stephen a millionaire.

The Best Investment Is a Four-Dimensional Investment!

Take some time to look at your investments, and see how many dimensions they employ. In the example of small businesses, the fourth dimension of investing can only be reached if you find a good manager to run it as efficiently as you can yourself. Also, many businesses are difficult to value, especially if they don't have any real assets like land or property. If the value of such a business does not go up, and if you cannot rely on a manager to run the business, then it will only be a two-dimensional investment.

In addition to this, if some businesses cannot leverage money to grow or expand, it will just be a one-dimensional investment. That said, one must remember that leverage is dangerous. Leverage should only be used if you are completely confident that you will be able to get a positive cash flow.

Leverage resulting in positive cash flow can make you rich.

Leverage resulting in negative cash flow can make you bankrupt.

There are many businesses that are only one dimensional. Such businesses can also be very successful if the profits are high, but if profits are poor, then it's going to be a constant struggle. Some people often wonder how guys like Stephen can be so successful. It's because their investment in their business is just one dimensional compared to Stephen's investment in rental properties which is four dimensional.

Ask yourself, "Are there any other dimensions I can add to increase my benefits?" Then take a little time right now to think about your next investment. How can you invest in a way that incorporates all four dimensions?

The Fifth Dimension of Property Investment

Property investment has a fifth dimension, which other investments rarely have. The fifth dimension is the ability to enjoy your property yourself. Imagine having a beachfront condo or vacation rental. It will give you all the benefits of four-dimensional property investment. But in addition to these four dimensions, you can enjoy the property yourself when you have no tenants.

You can have a free vacation on the beach during empty periods. You can enjoy it yourself and with your family and friends. You can't do this with your share certificates.

Property rental has the potential to provide you and your family with some happy moments and memories that are priceless, and that is on top of all the other benefits to your financial health.

Chapter 11

The Third Crisis
A Supersize Downsizing

'm sure you've heard it said that disagreements over money matters put one of the greatest strains on any loving relationship. When you are in the first stages of a new romance, the likelihood that you consider financial compatibility equal to love, chemistry, or sense of humor is pretty low. But as the relationship grows and develops, how you value the role of money in your life will become a greater factor. It is one of the leading contributors to divorce.

I learned the hard way that discussing finances and the value you and your partner place on fiscal responsibility is integral to any relationship. Without going into detail, I have been through a divorce. The breakdown of my marriage and our subsequent divorce was what I would call the third big crisis in my life.

When all the papers were signed, and I found myself alone again, I took a long look at how I should be living life now. I was back to making decisions on my own. As I looked at my post-divorce life, I knew that I was living in excess. I didn't need a three-bedroom home anymore. I didn't need half the things in my house.

After our very civilized parting, my ex-wife and I returned the things we had received from each other. This meant that I was now in possession of some diamond jewelry that I would never wear.

In my downsizing spree, I went back to the same store where we bought the diamonds, hoping to sell them. Of course, they offered a much lower price to buy it back. I checked other stores, but their offers were even worse. Those diamonds became a liability.

I had previously sold some land to buy the diamonds. The land I sold has now increased five times in value. Assets almost always increase in value. Lessons learned the hard way are difficult to forget.

> *Don't sell an asset to buy liability. Sell an asset only to buy another, a better asset.*

The first thing I did after my divorce was rent out my primary home and move back to my modest studio in the suburbs of Bangkok. When I did this, the volume of money I put into the process of doubling doubled. This enabled the volume of money put into the process of doubling to double without increasing any risk.

I'm going to use the example of Stephen again, but with parallels to my own experience, to show you what actually happened. Let's assume that like me, Stephen gets divorced at 35 and decides to rent his primary home and move into a little studio apartment.

By doing this, Stephen converts his primary home into an investment property. Now he will have two investment properties with a value of $325,000 each. He now has $650,000 in the process of doubling.

Stephen's Doubling Chart of Two Investment Properties At 8 Percent Return

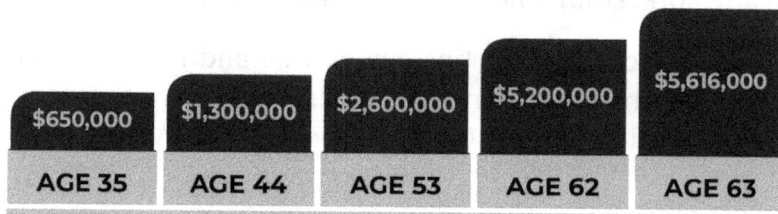

AGE 35	AGE 44	AGE 53	AGE 62	AGE 63
$650,000	$1,300,000	$2,600,000	$5,200,000	$5,616,000

By age sixty-three, the value of Stephen's investments has grown to $5,616,000! Now, the value of both these properties will be added to Stephen's net worth. We still must include appreciation on those properties. Stephen's doubling chart for appreciation is found below. (Remember that from the rule of 72, we know that the value of his investment properties will double every twenty-four years with 3 percent annual appreciation.)

Stephen's Doubling Chart of Two Investment Properties With 3 Percent Appreciation

$650,000 — AGE 35
$1,300,000 — AGE 59
$1,463,161 — AGE 63

With appreciation added to his investments, Stephen will have a net worth of $7,079,161.00 by the age of sixty-three! Seven million dollars by sixty-three, just because he decided to move out of his home to live in a studio after his divorce. The rent of the studio must be paid by Stephen from his active income; he must not use rental income received from investment properties to pay rent of the studio. This dramatic downsize—what I call a "supersize downsizing"—caused the volume of money that was put into the process of doubling to double, making Stephen a multimillionaire by retirement.

Frankly, not everybody can do this. It's hard to let go of so much. Remember I mentioned earlier that it's hard to downgrade? I was speaking from experience. It was hard for me to switch from my luxury condo with a swimming pool, squash court, badminton court, gymnasium, sauna, and masseuse to my studio apartment that had nothing. Nada. Zip. The only thing compelling me to downsize so drastically was this new life crisis. It was once again a catalyst, refocussing my energy and converting crisis into opportunity.

I had done the math. I knew that discomfort while I was still young would bring me comfort as I grew older. Knowing that this move would make me a multimillionaire made me more than happy to move to a small, cramped apartment for a time. I moved into that studio with a smile and watched my net worth grow as my rental income increased.

Something very important to note here is that making a decision like this is almost impossible unless you can envision that bright future for yourself. Our simple rule of 72 can give us this vision, and based on what we see in the future, we can make the right decisions today and act accordingly.

It's like traveling to the future and getting to know the winning lottery numbers and then traveling back to the present to buy that lottery ticket. Even if you are not able to achieve exactly what the rule of 72 shows you, you will still be miles ahead of where you would have been if you didn't head toward that goal.

You don't have to wait for a crisis to downsize and live below your means. Yes, super downsizing can help you get out of financial problems or bankruptcy faster, but it can also be used to accelerate your savings and investment plan.

I lived in that little studio apartment for a few years until I saved up enough money to buy another three-bedroom condo with a nice swimming pool and other amenities. I made sure to buy this new home and pay the mortgage from my active income only, not touching the rental income of the two investment properties. It only took a few years of hard work before I was back to my original lifestyle, and this new condo became my primary home. (The value of which I don't add to my net worth.)

As with the other previous crises in my life, divorce taught me many valuable lessons. Besides supersize downsizing, I discovered that there are three money personalities. There are *wealth creators, wealth preservers*, and *wealth spenders*.

Creators are the ones who create wealth through their business, investments, or talent. Self-made millionaires are wealth creators.

Preservers are conservative and careful with their money. Although they are not adept at creating much wealth, they create just enough to have a decent life and are good at preserving what they have or have inherited. They are cautious with their money and do not take too much risk.

Spenders, being true to their name, love to spend money. But they don't just spend money. They love to spend money—on liabilities, expensive vacations, and lavish lifestyles. These are the financially uneducated or undisciplined ones.

I have heard it said that the first generation are the creators of wealth, who, with hard work, sacrifice, and intelligence, create prosperity for themselves.

The second generation are preservers. If they cannot create wealth, at least they preserve what they have. The second generation tend to value the sacrifices of the first generation and are careful with their parents' money.

The third generation are the spenders, born millionaires. Their connection with the first generation and the hardships they endured are limited. By the third generation, the value of the effort put in by their grandparents is lost.

This is, of course, a generality. Not everyone fits into these categories, and personalities can change over time.

I believe it's vitally important to identify your financial personality and that of your partner. Are you a creator, preserver, or spender?

I am a first-generation wealth creator, and my ex-wife was a third-generation wealth spender. Creators have major difficulty living with spenders, whether they be a spouse, child, or roommate. It is much easier to live with a preserver because they understand and value the work of the creators and try their best to maintain the budgets they work on together.

Money was not the cause of my divorce, but money issues did add fuel to the fire. To avoid having a similar problem in my next marriage, I thought of a simple way to find out my own money personality and that of my future wife. With just a few simple questions, one can get an idea of what money personality the other has.

Have you ever bought anything with your money that has appreciated? Or have you ever bought an asset (other than your primary home) with your money?

If the answer is yes, then you are a potential creator of wealth. If the answer is no, then you are either a preserver or a spender of wealth.

Do you save money regularly, or do you have a habit of saving money every month?

If the answer is yes, then you are a potential preserver of wealth. If the answer is no, then you are a potential spender of wealth.

You may have found while reading that you yourself are a spender. You know that you can't pull out of the middle-class trap unless you become first a preserver and then a creator of wealth. Everything you need to create wealth is outlined here. But it will take discipline! Move slowly and steadily toward that goal, and you will find success.

Chapter 12

Volume and Risk

We live in an unstable world. Governments that seemed rock-solid have crumbled. Democracies are swinging from politically left to politically right. Businesses that seemed imperishable are going into bankruptcy. The feeling of instability is palpable. It infects every area of our lives—from work to business, investments, even our relationships.

The only thing certain today, as it has been for millennia, is death and taxes.

Life holds risk. No matter how you try and protect yourself, there will always be elements that are outside of your control. As life throws curve balls our way, we have two options: crumble under their weight or stand strong and learn from them.

In today's turbulent times, it is more important than ever to asses the risks that can affect our lives. It is vital we spend some time learning to protect ourselves and our families from all manner of challenges. Insurance can play an important role in protecting ourselves, but even insurance has its limits.

I am, in general, an optimist. I live my life and make financial decisions based on the assumption that I will live a long and full life, but I also believe it's important to think about protecting oneself from the unknown.

There are some things we can control. There are some decisions we make now that can help us and our family when we experience crisis. So take a minute to ask yourself, "What will happen to my assets and my family if tragedy befalls us?"

The concepts explained in this book are intended to make you financially secure. They assume that you will have long lives and die natural deaths. Since insurance will often only cover us until the age of sixty-five or seventy, I made this investment plan to protect and support myself and my family from retirement until the age of ninety or so. But these concepts also consider that while we are young and building our net worth, bad things can happen, and we need to protect ourselves from these uncertainties.

If you are the only earning member of your family, and no one else can pay that mortgage, I would highly suggest you invest in accident insurance and *remember to read* the fine print.

One way to lessen risk when you are young and invested in the future is to do all you can to climb back out of the middle-class trap and get your net worth back into the positive. My top priority must be to pay off my primary mortgage.

Once your primary mortgage is paid off, you can look at investing again, using your active income to expand your investments. This is when risk lessens. Using both active income and rental income together reduces the risk on your investment properties. It's wise to diversify our investments, if possible. This may mean purchasing property in other countries or at least in other communities or other forms of investments.

In addition to protecting yourself with insurance, it is wise to consider insuring extended family members as well, especially if later in life, it may fall to you to help with their care and expenses. It is important to manage your investment plan and debts to reduce risk and take on the responsibility of all your family members.

Health isn't the only risk we all must deal with; there are financial risks that cannot be controlled on a personal level. As I found out with the Asian Financial Crisis, economies can crash. You might lose tenants. You might lose your job. This is when how you choose to spend your active income becomes central.

Having a simple lifestyle and buying fewer liabilities will give you healthy savings and liquidity to weather this type of storm. Even if you borrow money to buy an asset, do not pay it down with the cash reserves you hold to save on interest. If you invest for positive cash flow, the interest on this borrowed money will be paid by the tenant, and you will have no need to worry about interest.

I probably don't need to say it again, but it's important enough that I'll repeat myself. Never spend a penny from your liquid assets for vacations, entertainment, or liabilities. Once you're are free from debt, you can live like a king, with no worries and with a positive net worth and positive cash flow, but until then, act wisely.

I always hold on to a certain amount of savings, which I never touch, even if it were to give me a lower interest in the bank. If you prefer to invest some portion of those savings and still keep them accessible, you may consider investing in gold, which is a more liquid asset.

The way I manage risk against the volume of money I invest can be thought about as a food pyramid. You remember those from health class, don't you? They would always have these food pyramid illustrations to show you how much of each food group you should be having to eat a well-balanced diet and live a healthy life.

At the base of the pyramid are all sorts of vegetables and a few grains. These foods offer the largest health benefits and can be consumed in higher volume than other foods. Next would come Fruits, legumes and nuts. They also provide great health benefits and can be consumed at a relatively high volume.

However, as you go higher on the pyramid, the benefits to your health decrease, and the risk increases. Because of this, the volume of food you can eat in each category decreases the further up the pyramid you go. The next step could be protein in the form of fish and lean meat. At the tip would be sugar and fried stuff. You would be posing a significant risk to your health if you ate more sugar and deep-fried foods than vegetables, fruits, and grains.

This is much the same way I manage my financial health. I weigh the benefit versus risk and adjust the volume of money I invest accordingly—investing the largest volume of my money where the risk is the lowest.

At the base of my financial pyramid is property investment. This is where I will put my maximum money. For me, property is low-risk, so it will become the base foundation of my investment. As I go up the pyramid, the volume of money I budget will decrease as the risk goes up.

The next level of investment for me would be blue-chip stocks, where the volume is lower, but the risk is a little higher. For some, it may be the other way, with the largest amount of their budget being invested in stocks and property investment becoming the second tier.

This is dependent on how one assesses risk and their knowledge and ability to invest. Business owners will have the highest volume of money invested in their business as they know their business well and earn a higher return on their money investing in their own business rather than properties and stocks. So, for business owners, the base of their pyramid will be their business.

After properties and stocks, the next tier could be cash. Cash can be kept in the form of your local currency or foreign currencies like the Swiss Frank, or a part can be invested in gold. And while investing in lower-risk stock options won't bring you big cash right away, it does have a better possibility of long-term gain.

Perhaps the next tier might be investing in insurance, which, as we saw above, is a worthwhile and important investment to protect yourself and your assets. As you go higher, the volume of money invested decreases further until we get to the small amount of money budgeted for buying liabilities and vacations.

At the tip of the pyramid, the volume is the lowest, the risk highest. Perhaps you are someone who likes to play the lottery or want to try your luck at the casino or with a riskier stock investment or cryptocurrencies.

Let's call the tip of the pyramid, "Las Vegas." This is the very small volume of money I would use on riskier investments. Only take the small amount of money you can afford to lose, which will not affect your life in any way, and go ahead and gamble on an investment. It's such a small amount. Win or lose, you can have some fun with it.

If "Las Vegas" is at the base of your pyramid rather than the tip, you are in big trouble. The last thing I want is for one of my readers to learn the concept of doubling and gamble with their hard-earned money to try doubling it.

Gamble on high-risk investments but only with the small amount of money at the tip of the pyramid and not the base investment amount.

Everyone's budget is different depending on their net worth. But the structure of the pyramid remains the same. If you have a net worth of billions, then budgeting a billion at the base and gambling with a million dollars at the tip will not be a big deal.

But if you have a net worth of over a million, then perhaps your base investments will be only $600,000, and you should only budget a $1000, with which to gamble. (Personally, I would only gamble with a $100 if I have a net worth of a million.)

If you have a negative net worth and have borrowed significantly, you do not have enough money with which to gamble at all.

On the next page is an example of Stephen's risk-versus-volume pyramid. Keep in mind that this pyramid is the amount of money invested after he has paid for his necessities and primary home. Basically, this pyramid represents a healthy way to manage your money and increase your net worth.

Risk-Versus-Volume Pyramid

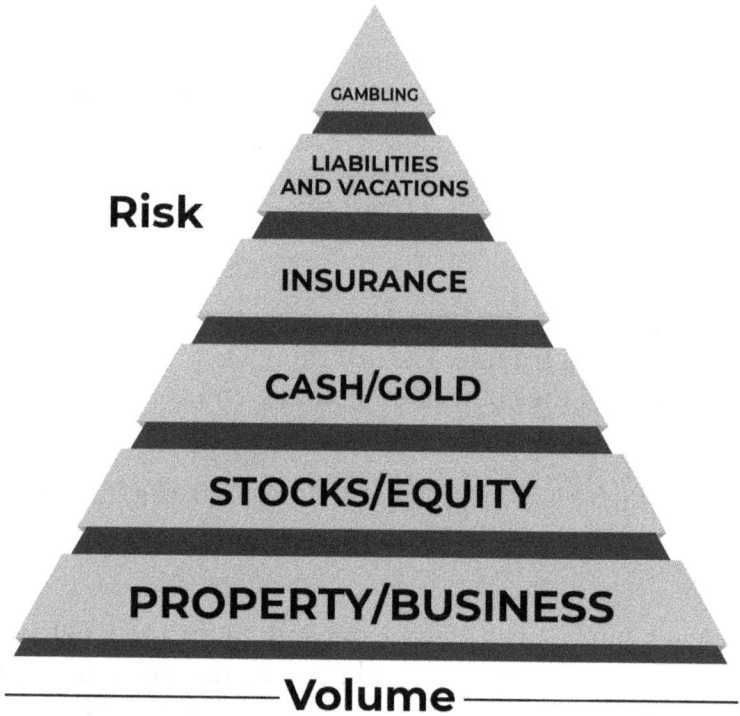

On the next page is a pyramid for you to fill in yourself. Be honest about your budget. This will help you to see how you are managing your risks. Where have you invested the maximum amount of your money? Put this at the bottom of the pyramid, and as you go up the pyramid, fill in the blanks to see where you are investing your money.

My Risk-Versus-Volume Pyramid

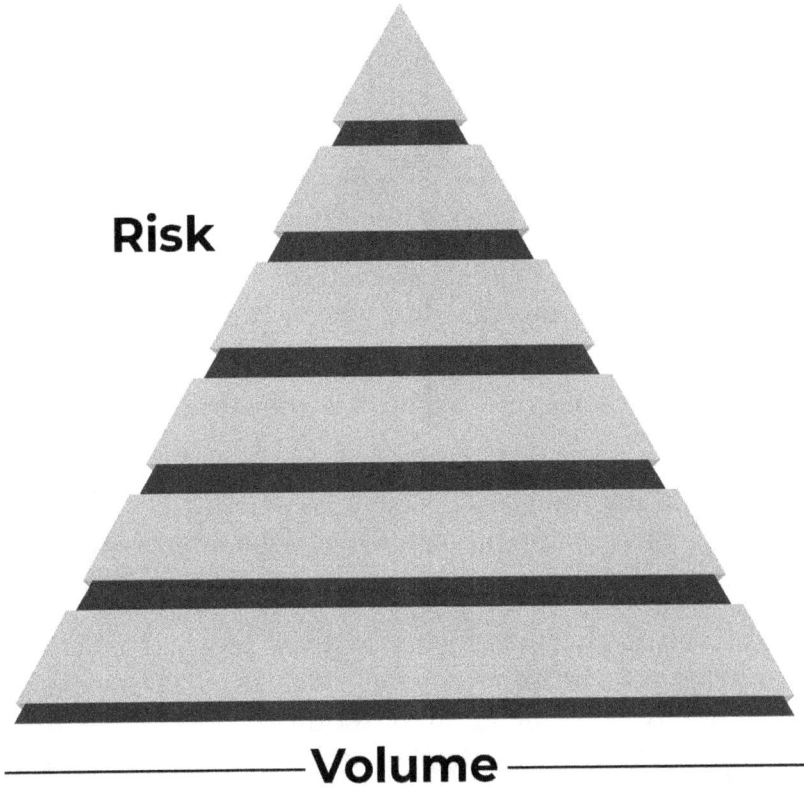

Risk

Volume

There is another risk that we haven't yet discussed. Stephen might not be able to invest at an 8 percent return on his money for the long term. If Stephen can't get that minimum 8 percent return for the duration of his investment, he won't be able to compound his investments as quickly, and his net worth at sixty-three would be less than $3.5 million.

Even with the 8 percent "sure thing" that I look diligently for, there is the risk that it will drop. It has happened to me on occasion. If I aim for 8 percent, it can drop to 7 or 6 percent return.

But if you were to aim only for a 6 percent return, then it could drop to 5 or 4 percent, and the time it takes to double your investment grows significantly. So what do we do in such cases?

Of course, we try to buy properties that will give us a higher return, but this is not always possible. If the return on existing property drops, there are ways to try to increase the return, like making home improvements and renting at a higher price after the refurbishing is done or renting out short-term on *Airbnb* and similar other platforms. But if this does not work, then the only

> **If a return drops in interest, then the volume of money invested must be increased to achieve the same net worth.**

option is to increase the volume of money invested to achieve the same net worth.

We saw the importance of money volume in the concept of doubling—the greater the volume of money you invest, the fewer number of cycles will be required to double your money.

How do you accrue more money to invest? It can be increased by growing your active income or increasing your savings and investing this extra amount to offset the drop in return. As we also saw in the previous chapter, downsizing will also play an important role if it can be done.

Another way to increase the volume is to sell a current asset for an asset of even greater value. Remember when I had mentioned that appreciation is not that important? At this point, if you decide to sell your asset to buy a bigger asset, then appreciation will become of greater importance, but the risk will also increase as you borrow higher amounts of money to buy a superior asset.

Let's look once more at the example of Stephen's first investment property. He bought it at $325,000 at the age of thirty-five. He got an 8 percent return enabling him to double his money in nine years. Let's assume that he is able to pay off his debt in nine years to understand the concept. So by the time Stephen is forty-four, he will have a debt-free property with a value of $424,000, including appreciation (appreciation at 3 percent per annum).

This means that, theoretically, after nine years, Stephen can put down this $424,000 as a 20 percent down payment to buy a property with a value of $2,120,000. The volume of money put into the process of doubling has increased dramatically, but the amount of debt has also increased.

However, later, when these two-million-dollar properties are paid off, the money it makes can be put down as a 20 percent down payment on a 10-million-dollar property. And when this 10-million-dollar property is paid off, it can be used as a 20 percent down payment for a 50-million-dollar property. This is how the rich make money and become richer.

Many rich people overborrow and live most of their life on borrowed money. Unfortunately some of them wind up bankrupt when the economy takes a sudden downturn.

When the volume of money invested increases, the risk also increases and must be managed well to avoid problems and bankruptcy. The only way they can be successful is when the economy is doing well, and all their investments are positive-cash-flowing investments.

For those who cannot increase their income and choose to increase their savings, the best way to save money is to buy in volume at cheaper prices. The concept of risk and volume can be applied to necessities, liabilities, and assets also.

Both liabilities and assets can be bought in a higher volume to save you money. Clothes and shoes or even vacations, if combined with large groups of people, can be bought at a lower cost to increase savings. Getting together with friends or family and creating an investment group will allow you to buy large properties or many properties at a lower price due to the higher volume.

Your negotiating power goes up, which, in turn, helps reduce the purchase price, resulting in higher returns on your investments. There is risk involved in these types of investing groups too, and it is imperative that the group has clear goals and vision in place as well as contracts signed between the members to outline the financial responsibility of each member. This is important even if it is family investing together.

Chapter 13

Financial Freedom

"**F**reeee-dom!"

It's the kind of word that you shout like the courageous, kilted Mel Gibson in *Braveheart*. The word *freedom* conjures up images of courage under fire. It is synonymous with valor, liberty, and independence.

But for some reason, when you link freedom with finances, it loses some of its sexy imagery. No matter how many Freedom 55 commercials you watch with grey-haired couples cuddling on sailboats, "financial freedom" brings to mind images of pale-faced men sitting in stamp-sized offices, droning on and on about budgets and compound interest.

I wish I could change that for you. I wish the words *financial freedom* made you want to stand up and fight for your future. For that to happen, you need to choose it. Just like the men in *Braveheart*, you have to want it. You may have to be willing to give up some of the luxuries you have grown accustomed to, but is it worth it? Yeah, it is!

William Shakespeare famously wrote, "All the world is a stage, and all the men and women merely players." But I like to think of life more like playing a video game. We aren't just characters acting out scenes with a well-constructed outcome. We are managing crises, fighting the bad guy, finding our way through new landscapes.

The early levels, though difficult at first, feel easy once you've mastered the techniques you need to beat them. Once you reach the higher levels, it is like a whole new game. You've gained skills and experience points. You've armed yourself well. You may have found secret doors to help you skip levels.

But in each higher level, the enemy is stronger and bigger than before. You know that to win, to get the real treasure or defeat the enemy, you will need to face the big boss. It is only if you defeat him that you will win the game.

Every crisis I faced was like a bad guy in my life. Once I had "killed the bad guy" or had overcome each crisis, it presented me with a key to the next level of understanding and riches. I gained experience and skill that would enable me to face the next crisis better equipped than I had been before.

I thought that being a multimillionaire was the end goal of the game. In the beginning of my financial education, it was that which was uppermost in my mind. I was sure that if I had millions of dollars, I was winning, but I was wrong.

As I learned about the concept of supersize downsizing, I discovered a key that opened a door to a secret level. A new wisdom, which I would say is far more important than being a millionaire.

The first time I lived in a studio apartment, it was out of necessity rather than choice. However, when I moved back to the studio apartment, it was because I chose to downsize. I could have remained in one of the two luxury three-bedroom investment properties I owned, but that would mean forfeiting one really good rental income each month.

Because I chose to live a simple lifestyle, my expenses were low. At the same time, the total rent I received from my rental properties was much higher. When I realized that my passive income from the apartments was much higher than my monthly expenses, I felt liberated. This meant that I no longer needed to work to cover my expenses. If I wanted to, I could live my life from the passive income I was receiving in the form of rent.

Unlike the imaginary Stephen, who bought an investment property at full value when he was thirty-five, I managed to buy my first property at the age of twenty-eight for under the market value. The luxury three-bedroom apartment I bought was listed at one-third of its value, because of the Asian Financial crisis. This allowed me to pay off the debt on my primary property very quickly.

I also did not have much debt on the second property. In fact, at that point, I had enough cash reserves to pay off the debt on both properties, but as I said before, it is important to reserve your savings for emergencies. If I had paid off these debts, I would have emptied my savings and been low on liquidity. But knowing that I had the cash necessary to pay off all my debts made me feel free.

You don't always realize the burdens you are carrying until they are gone. This took away all my financial-related stress. Financial freedom meant that I could retire at thirty-five and live off the rent from the two properties. If I quit my job, I could travel the world. I could see and experience things that others only dream about. This financial freedom is usually only the privilege of the rich, but I managed to achieve it by thirty-five, not fifty-five, like the commercials tout. I was still in my thirties. Freedom 35!

> **Put simply, when your passive income is higher than the total expenses of your desired lifestyle, you are financially free.**

An amazing thing happens to your mentality about work when you know you don't actually need employment. I didn't quit my job and travel the world. I quite liked my job, and it allowed me to travel quite often anyway, but I went to work now because I wanted to work. Despite the relief and freedom that I felt, I didn't lose sight of the fact that I was only able to accomplish this feat by choosing to live a very simple lifestyle. If I had chosen to be single for the rest of my life and didn't need to provide for anyone but myself, I might have moved back home to India and never needed to work again. But there were four good reasons I did not choose this insanely early retirement.

Reason 1: Although I was financially free, it was a very basic financial freedom. It felt great, but the lifestyle I was living was not my desired lifestyle. I desired more. I wanted to live at a higher level of financial freedom, and for that, I would have to continue to work and increase my passive income.

Reason 2: If I retired, I would not have any active income, which meant that I would have to start using my rental income for expenses. Doing this would mean that I wouldn't be able to compound my investments and double them as quickly as I had planned and predicted.

Reason 3: All the passive income that I generated was the result of my active income. So, for me, sustaining my active income while I was young was more important than having my passive income sustain me. By investing my time into developing both incomes, I would bring in the highest income possible.

Reason 4: Most importantly, my aim was never to be financially free by thirty-five. My real vision was to be financially free when I could no longer bring in an active income and to continue to be financially free well into my nineties.

If becoming a multimillionaire is your only goal, there will be no end to your desire to make money. If your goal is to show others how successful you are or to keep up with the Joneses and move in the best circles, you will not experience freedom.

Your finances will always control your thinking and cause you stress. If your goal is to hang out with successful business owners, you will only be satisfied when you have an equally successful business. If your desired goal is to be able to go on vacations with millionaires and celebrities, you will need to have millions at hand to afford the same lifestyle.

Many business owners, millionaires, and celebrities are not financially free. They need their businesses or active income to pay the expenses of their lavish lifestyle. They haven't built a stream of passive income; instead, they try to keep building more active incomes.

Big business owners who are successful have nothing to worry about. They can hire good managers who can run their business efficiently in their absence. Big businesses who have healthy profits compound their investments by investing in their own businesses. If the business saturates and cannot grow due to poor economic conditions, they diversify and invest their profits into lower-return investments like apartments, hotels, or office buildings, which are also passive businesses.

Many small business owners are successful too, and like big businesses, they are also able to create passive incomes, but on a smaller scale. But some small business owners are not as successful. I know many small business owners who are still struggling. In a highly competitive world with rapidly advancing technology, they are constantly reinventing themselves to stay ahead.

I, on the other hand, was financially free, though I was "only an employee." By choosing to live a simpler lifestyle and managing my money well, I didn't have the same stress that many of these people had.

The key is focus.

Is your focus on financial freedom, or is it on "being your own boss?" So many people, tired of working the nine-to-five grind, make being their own boss the goal. They believe they will feel free if they just don't have to report to the manager.

If people shifted their focus away from being their own boss to financial freedom, they would develop the kind of thinking that is needed to create passive income, and passive income is the only way to really achieve this sort of freedom.

Don't get me wrong. I am not suggesting that being an employee is better than being a business owner. Of course, being a business owner is always better, but not every business owner is successful. If you open a viable business and use the active income from it for investments that build a passive income, you will have the best of both worlds.

Are you financially free? Was that even a goal for you? To find out, you need to ask yourself the following two questions:

What are the total monthly expenses to sustain my lifestyle? (Think carefully. Add up all your expenses, and note them down in the chart below.)

How much monthly passive income do I earn? (Add up any passive income you receive. This might include rental income, dividends from stocks, and monthly interest received from fixed deposits in the bank. Add them all up, minus any monthly debts you owe, and write the amount down in the chart below.)

Financial Freedom Chart

MY MONTHLY EXPENSES	MY MONTHLY PASSIVE INCOME	MINUS MONTHLY DEBT
$	$	$
$	$	$
$	$	$
$	$	$
$	$	$

Are you financially free? If so, congratulations! If not, it's time to shift your focus from less important things in your life and look toward achieving financial freedom. You have now studied the concepts necessary to achieve this, but even if you have read every word—from cover to cover multiple times—even if you believe it wholeheartedly, they will do you no good unless you start to follow them.

Business owners must ask themselves, "If I stopped working, can my business run as efficiently and profitably in my absence?" If you find that it can run on its own, congratulations! You have passive business income, and you are already enjoying the best of both worlds.

Once I tasted financial freedom and knew just how sweet it is, I wanted to achieve it at a level that could support more than just myself living frugally in a studio apartment for the rest of my life.

I wanted to have a family and children and a bigger home. It is a good thing I didn't go crazy as soon as I learned my passive income was enough to sustain me. It's a great thing that I enjoyed my work. My continued active income from work meant that I could continue to invest and earn more passive income.

If you feel like you will never manage to have a secure financial future because buying two properties by thirty-five is impossible for you, I want to point out again that switching your focus to financial freedom can still lead you to the place you want to be in your retirement.

Buying two properties with a value of $650,000 by the age of thirty-five is just an example. As we saw in the last chapter, the important thing to understand is how to manage the volume of money invested against the risk the investment holds.

If you happen to be reading this book and are living in a smaller town in North America, Europe, or in a developing country, the dollar amounts listed won't even be close to what you can expect to earn.

Purchasing two properties at $325,000 each would take a lifetime to afford. There are many places where that amount of money would buy you a mansion. If that is where you are living, I hope you haven't become disheartened. The important thing is to learn these concepts and apply them to smaller volumes of money.

As the cost of living in smaller towns and cities (or in developing countries) is much lower, the volume of money needed to invest is a fraction of what it would be in a place like New York. I know we have talked a lot about becoming a millionaire by retirement, but that number is set as an example. It is not meant to be a fixed score that will win you the game. This isn't tennis—no need to be disheartened. You have an equal chance to become financially free and live an equally good lifestyle.

Simplification, or living a simple lifestyle, can help you bring down the costs for retirement. You have seen how Stephen, due to simplification, was able to retire a millionaire. Stephen had simplified his life at every stage to achieve this. He didn't buy a car when he first got his job; he chose to take public transport and save money. Later, he chose to live in a smaller home and used the remainder of his money to buy an investment property.

It was the money saved from living a simpler life and investing his money wisely that made him a millionaire. With Stephen's simple formula, there was no chance that he won't be a millionaire by the time he retires.

If you practice the same principles, then you too can be guaranteed millionaires by the time you retire. What Stephen did was not very hard; he just lived simply, saved as much as possible, invested wisely, and compounded his investments.

We know that Stephen becomes a millionaire by retirement, but does he achieve financial freedom?

Let's first look at Stephen's passive income by the time he's sixty-three. Cash flow or rental income is what we need when we retire. At sixty-three, Stephen continues to get an income from his investment properties, and this contributes to his passive income.

We are calculating his passive income from his investment properties ($2,808,000 with 8 percent returns) and not his net worth ($3,551,576) because we are calculating the return only on the amount he has invested and not on the appreciated value of the property.

If we calculate an 8 percent return on $2,808,000, then his annual rental income will be $224,640. The rent of the properties Stephen bought when he was thirty-five will surely increase by the time he reaches his sixties. In fact, that rental return will increase by more than 8 percent of the purchase price, but to simplify things, we won't consider this increase; we'll just stick to that 8 percent average.

A rental income of $224,640 per year or $18,720 per month, even with inflation, should be more than sufficient for Stephen to retire and be financially free.

Some of you may want to have financial freedom but can't imagine living a frugal life. Maybe you know that you enjoy luxuries too much to really give them up. If so, there is another option to the supersize downsizing. This again applies more to people living in the western world or expensive countries like Japan, Hongkong and Singapore.

Moving to a developing country, where lifestyle expenses are much lower, may be just what you need to be financially free faster.

That taste of financial freedom I experienced at thirty-five stayed with me. It was my new goal. Although my expenses were increased (I had moved to a new three-bedroom condo), my rental income also increased. I was able to compound the passive income received from both my investment properties by buying more properties with that rental income, maintaining my state of financial freedom.

I got married and had a daughter and a son, which increased my expenses further. But by this point, compounding was working in my favor. My rental income continued to bring in a larger passive income. Even today, I have never needed to spend a penny from my rental income on my living expenses. Every bit of my passive income is reinvested and put into the process of doubling. I was also able to manage my debt in such a way that even though I had loans, I could maintain my financially free status. I still have mortgages with the bank and continue to borrow money to buy more investment properties, but despite having these loans, I am still financially free.

To achieve this, maintaining or increasing my active income was crucial. Strong active income means I could buy some smaller properties in cash, increase my net worth, as well as reduce my debt, enhance my cash flow, and reduce risk. Less risk plus more cash flow made me unafraid to buy more and more properties. My active and passive incomes working together help me maintain my financially free state even as my expenses increase.

I know in past chapters that I have gone on and on about not spending money on liabilities and vacations. I am sure you must think they are the destroyers of all things good. But let me assure you that I love vacations and liabilities as much as the next guy. I never meant for you never to take vacations or spend money on stuff you like, but if we live it up while we are young with no thought to the future, we are inviting tough times to visit us when we're older. It's important to strike that balance between enjoyment and fiscal responsibility. Therein lies freedom!

Chapter 14

Beating Inflation

As a kid, I was fascinated by stories my grandfather told of how cheap stuff was in his day. When my grandparents were just married, they could get a plate of mutton biryani for just ₹2.50 (rupees), which is equal to 4¢. Today, that same mutton biryani would cost ₹400 rupees, or $6.50.

I am sure you must have heard your grandparents saying things like, "Times sure have changed. In my day, you could buy a Coca-Cola for 5¢!"[5]

For many of us, hearing stories of "the good old days" was our first introduction to the concept of inflation, although most of us never actually heard the term until we learned about it in school. It was hardly a fun learning experience.

School textbooks often describe inflation this way: "The rate at which the general level of prices for goods and services is rising and, consequently, the purchasing power of currency is falling. Central banks attempt to limit inflation, and avoid deflation, to keep the economy running smoothly."[6]

It's fascinating to look back at how prices have inflated over the last century, but have you ever taken some time to think about what the price of staple goods and services might rise to when we reach retirement age?

I did a little experiment using an inflation calculator. I wanted

---

[5] In 1940, a bottle of Coca-Cola cost 5¢ and a loaf of bread 10¢.
[6] http://www.investopedia.com/terms/i/inflation.asp

to know what a loaf of bread might cost in forty-five years. It's a little scary.

I estimated that an average white loaf today costs around $1.95. In forty-five years, it is estimated to cost—drumrolls—$12.10! That is at an average inflation rate of 4.14 percent—4 percent doesn't sound so high, and 4 percent is barely anything, right?

But those pennies add up, and they compound. Therefore, the price of bread is going to be six times the present price in forty-five years.

If a loaf of bread will cost six times the price, over $12 when you retire, what will happen to your hard-earned savings? Will being a millionaire be enough? The world is changing quickly. There is an increasing sense of insecurity, and now, I tell you that you won't be able to afford bread forty-some years from now.

Of course, we know that as inflation makes the cost of living increase, governments work to ensure our living wage increases as well. When governments institute an increase in minimum wage, businesses must pay employees more. To do that, they need to charge more for their goods or services, creating the cycle we are talking about.

After becoming financially free, I believed I was financially wise, but I hadn't factored in inflation. When the Thai government suddenly increased minimum labor charges by 50 percent, the price of everything skyrocketed. The sudden increase in my expenses threatened my financial freedom. The rental income from my apartments was no longer enough to cover my cost of living.

Imagine going on a vacation to a foreign destination without knowing how much it's going to cost you. You imagine that the cost of living is the same in every developed country, so you plan a three-month vacation to Europe with a €1000 in your pocket. At home, this would cover a hotel, meals, and other incidentals.

You have no doubt that €1000 is all you need. The truth is that many tourists get stranded abroad on vacations because they run out of money. Instead of a villa for next to nothing and locals begging to have them over for meals, they find that even a hostel is more expensive than a hotel back in their hometown. Reality bites hard. Phone calls are made home, and money wired from worried friends and family.

You don't want to be one of those people, do you? Retirement is sometimes called the long vacation. And if all goes well, it really will be like the longest vacation of your life. But if you go into it unprepared, without knowing how much money you really need, you will find yourself scraping by and looking for someone to bail you out of your predicament.

Understanding the concept of inflation is the only way to make accurate predictions on what you will need to be financially free in your retirement years.

So how do we preserve the value of our money? We need to

> Let's say we hide $10,000 away in savings. If there is on an average a 5 percent inflation on most goods and services every year, then after just one year, the value of that money would be the equivalent of $9,500. That is quite a loss.

invest it at a higher rate than the rate of inflation in the country we are living in.

Thomas was more interested in travel and adventure than investing. He kept $10,000 in a savings account at a rate of interest of 2 percent. Now, if we assume that inflation was very low at 2 percent, and Thomas gets 2 percent interest in the bank, then the value of his $10,000 in savings at the age of seventy-one will still be only $10,000.

Just like interest compounds, inflation also compounds. Although the dollar amount of Thomas's savings will be $20,000 when he is seventy-one, the actual value of that money will be less. He will still only have the equivalent of $10,000 when he is seventy-one.

Because of Thomas's spending habits, he wasn't able to save enough money to ensure his financial security in retirement. Not that Thomas was the type to be interested in investing anyway. He's a live-for-the-moment type of guy. Unfortunately for Thomas, his disinterest in investments and the low rate of return on his savings mean that he will be put in a very difficult situation upon his retirement.

Our old friend Stephen will obviously fair better, but is he really going to beat inflation? As you saw, there are some sharp increases over the course of forty or fifty years.

For this example, let's assume that the rate of inflation in America isn't quite as high as in some other countries. How does 3 percent sound? Let's also assume that at thirty-five, Stephen needs around $2000 a month to live a comfortable life. This allows Stephen to eat healthy, buy new clothes when he needs them, go out with friends, cover any medical expenses, travel a little, and take a vacation abroad once a year.

With this $2000 a month, he happily lives his desired lifestyle. He is so content with his current way of life that he hopes to sustain it in his retirement. This means that Stephen's expenses each year, not counting housing, will be $24,000. I know you've missed seeing my doubling charts, so I've made one for Stephen with a 3 percent inflation rate.

Remember the rule of 72? It tells us that 3 percent inflation will double Stephen's expenses every twenty-four years (72/3 = 24).

Doubling Chart For Stephen's Lifestyle Expense With 3 Percent Inflation

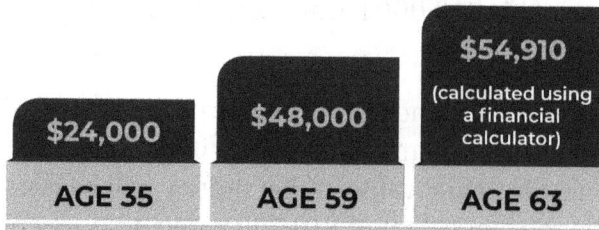

$24,000 — AGE 35
$48,000 — AGE 59
$54,910 (calculated using a financial calculator) — AGE 63

This means, that for Stephen to maintain his current lifestyle at 63, he'll be spending $54,910 every year. After retirement, Stephen won't have any more active income, and he will depend solely on his investments to cover his expenses.

Because Stephen invested wisely and aimed for an 8 percent return, we can assume that he has beaten inflation, since he was able to invest at a higher rate than the rate of inflation. But let's play this whole scenario out to see just how comfortable and secure he can be in retirement.

The World Economic Forum recently came out with a report that they expect there to be a $400 trillion shortfall in retirement savings. They say that with advances in science and medicine, people are living longer, but expected retirement age hasn't changed—meaning the shortfall will continue to grow. Moreover, employers have moved away from pensions and are instead offering 401(k)s and individual retirement accounts.[7]

With these statistics in mind, let's assume that Stephen will live until he's ninety. That gives Stephen twenty-seven years to enjoy his retirement. This also means that toward the end of those years, there will be a decrease in travel and vacation and entertainment expenses but an increase in medical expenses. This will likely balance out his spending, so we will stick with our estimated $54,910 yearly. So let's do the math! $54,910 x 27 years = $1,482,570 (total expenses)

Most people would calculate this far and then aim for this lump sum figure to secure their retirement. But this would be wrong. Firstly, we already know this figure is wrong because continued inflation will make expenses increase every year of Stephen's retirement. Secondly, this kind of thinking limits you. A lump sum amount saved to sustain you in your retirement is not thinking holistically. If you only plan this far, you will likely run out of money in your old age.

---

[7] http://www.bangkokpost.com/news/general/1257034/retire-ment-savings-time-bomb-ticking

I am going to add 3 percent inflation to Stephen's annual expenses from the age of sixty-three to ninety and then add it all up. We will also compare Stephen's passive income at the age of sixty-three to the expense of his desired lifestyle at that age.

MONEY STEPHEN NEEDS TO RETIRE PER YEAR AT 3 PERCENT INFLATION		STEPHEN'S PASSIVE INCOME AT 8 PERCENT. RETURN AT AGE 63.	
AGE		**AGE**	
63	$54,910.00	63	$224,640.00
68	$63,655.73		
73	$73,794.44		
78	$85,547.98		
83	$99,173.56		
88	$114,969.33		
90	$121,970.96		
(annually)			

If we add up these annual expenses, the total comes to $2,357,336! Can you believe it! That is almost a million dollars more than previously calculated. It's just enough to live with the same level of comfort he has grown accustomed to before his retirement years.

My wife often tells me how rich her grandparents used to be in the olden days. Her grandfather was very wealthy, but she and her siblings grew up middle-class, and she doesn't understand what happened.

"There are three reasons why you and your siblings are middle-class despite having rich grandparents," I told her.

First of all, her grandfather had five children, and her father had eight. That's the fastest way to divide your inheritance. Her grandfather's wealth was already divided by five, her father's portion by eight. What would be left of her grandfather's wealth if it got divided forty times in two generations?

Secondly, things don't cost what they once did. Inflation can easily make the rich into the middle-class of the future. If inflation decreases the value of the inheritance, six times in two generations, their grandfather's wealth, already divided forty times, will be divided six more times.

That's 240 times it has been divided in two generations. So, if her grandfather had a net worth of $10 million in cash at the time of his passing, her inheritance would only be $41,666.

And the third reason why her family had less than her grandparents is that none of them were creators of wealth. They weren't even preservers of wealth, except for my wife. Most of them were spenders. This is how the rich of today can be the middle-class of the future.

Exactly the opposite happened to many families in some parts of China. The world criticized China for being undemocratic and enforcing the one-child policy. And yes, there are many disadvantages of having only one child, but after a few generations, this sacrifice made by some of the Chinese people has created a very wealthy generation of Chinese. They have not only created a wealthy generation but have also taken masses out of poverty. Let me explain what happened.

When a child is born, he inherits money from both his parents. Since he does not have to share the inheritance with a sibling, he receives both the share. Later, this child marries another person, who is also an only child and has inherited from both parents.

Together, this couple has one child who inherits four times over. The generation after this inherits eight times what they might have. Also, a single child means fewer expenses and more savings to invest.

The Chinese multiplied their wealth with the one-child policy. Additionally, because of the tremendous economic opportunities in China for work and business, many became creators of wealth. These creators of wealth and sole inheritors have resulted in a generation of very rich Chinese citizens, who are traveling and buying properties worldwide, driving the tourism industry and property prices very high in countries like the U.S., Canada, and Australia.

It is sometimes hard to see the things your family is doing that causes financial instability when you are used to living a lavish lifestyle. Those who are used to living in luxury will think that buying chicken instead of steak is a real sacrifice or going to a four-star rather than a five-star resort for their summer holidays is living frugally.

> **Being a spender, coupled with inflation, over time will make the rich become middle-class and the middle-class become poor.**

Let's assume a rich kid, aged thirty-five, has gotten used to living on $5,000 a month and only hangs out with people who live a similar lifestyle. If he has neither learned to be a creator of wealth nor a preserver, he will quickly blow through his money and will really experience hardship by the time he reaches retirement.

This spending habit could change if this person knew that a $5000 lifestyle expense when you are 35 translates to an expense of $5,893,342 from the age of sixty-three to ninety with 3 percent inflation. If inflation is higher, then the expense could be much higher. A person who does not know this will continue to spend and could face trouble in the future, especially if he has not planned for this $5,893,342 expense.

Our plan here isn't to have a $2 million golden goose that we hope sustains us until we die. Our plan is to have a goose that lays golden eggs. The golden eggs will sustain us until we die, and the goose will be passed on to our children. We want to have a plan that provides a sustainable passive income. Stephen's investments are exactly that, so he really has nothing to worry about.

You can see from our chart that his passive income is always more than his expenses. He could live to 102, and he will still have more passive income than he needs. This is the true financial freedom we were talking about in the last chapter. Stephen has enough passive income to take it easy and relax for the rest of his life. More than that, he has enough assets that he will be able to pass them on to future generations.

If you are used to living frugally, it might look like Stephen has way more passive income than he needs, but remember that there is always the possibility, especially as you grow older, of greater medical expenses. Pensions and government assistance for senior citizens are often not enough to ensure a good quality of life, and so I'd say that this is still a "safe" goal.

Additionally, we saw in the chapter of risk and volume that it's possible that Stephen will not be able to get an 8 percent return on all his investments for his entire life. So if the return drops, resulting to a passive income drop, he still has a comfortable margin to be financially free until he dies.

The chart below can make it easy for you to decide on the type of lifestyle you want to get used to so that you don't have to cut back when you are older. You might have to for other reasons, but finances shouldn't be one of them.

MONTHLY LIFESTYLE EXPENSES AT AGE 35	YEARLY EXPENSES AT AGE 63 WITH 3% INFLATION	MONEY REQUIRED TO LIVE FROM AGE 63 TO 90 WITH 3% INFLATION
$1000	$27,455	$1,178,668
$2000	$54,910	$2,357,336
$3000	$82,365	$3,536,005
$4000	$109,820	$4,714,673
$5000	$137,275	$5,893,342

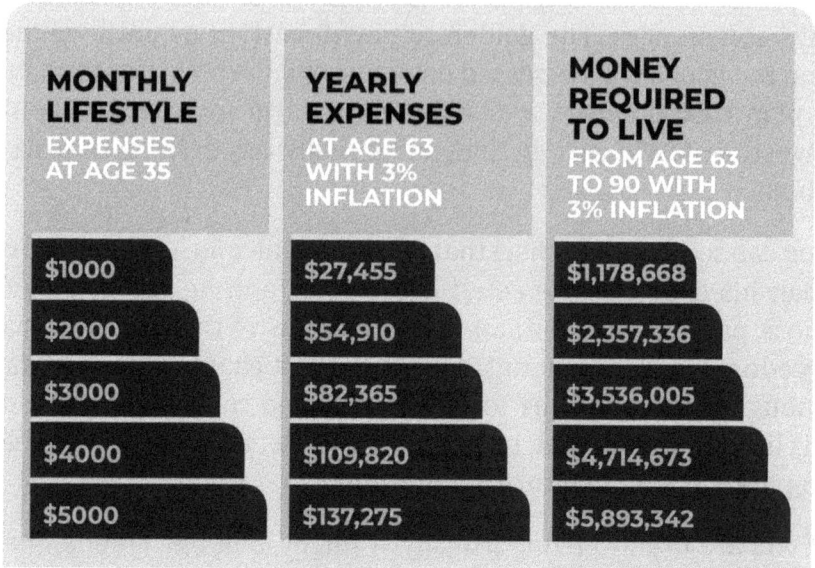

Does that help you see how much money you'll require to retire depending on the lifestyle you choose? If inflation in your country is higher, then this figure will be much higher. So be wise in choosing your lifestyle expenses as I mentioned before. Downgrading yourself is hard to do.

What is the key point to remember to beat inflation? That is to invest at a rate higher than the rate of inflation!

It is easy to find out the inflation rate in the area you live and check that your investments are yielding a higher return than the rate of inflation.

Ask yourself, "What am I prepared to do to achieve permanent financial freedom for myself and my family? Am I moving in the right direction to achieve this permanent freedom?"

Chapter 15

My Financial Journey Continues, and Yours Too
Predict your Financial Future
(Part 2)

'**ve invested and grown rich; however, it wasn't easy. Despite doing well with my initial property purchases in Thailand, I had almost messed things up later with some bad decisions because I didn't know much of the country yet. I was a foreigner and I made some mistakes, which cost me money.

Mistakes can be too damaging and set you back years in your journey toward financial freedom. Luckily, the mistakes I made didn't affect me significantly. Even though the loss was quite a lot, I was able to get back on track and *learn* from my mistakes.

I realized that *only knowing the concepts* was not enough. One must do *thorough research* in choosing the right property to buy and invest in. So take advantage if you're living in your own country as you know the place well.

Unlike me, who was alone, you have family, friends and might have connections with people in the real estate business whom you can ask for help in knowing the best rental properties to buy. Having that kind of support plus these concepts here can help you achieve bigger success than mine.

After having a long journey filled with many ups and downs, I have finally become financially free. I'm happy that I started investing early long before having a family. This helped me built a steady, healthy stream of passive income on top of my strong active income. This combination enabled me to support the expenses of having two children and keep my savings and investments well above water.

My sacrifices when I was younger have paid off big-time. Now, my family and I have moved from the suburbs and settled back into downtown Bangkok, back to the first apartment I had bought during the Asian crisis. This apartment was always my home, which I decided to leave after my first divorce, in my downsizing spree.

The rent I received from this apartment right from the start was not only enough to cover the cost of the apartment but also for the renovations I had to do before moving to live there myself. So we now live in a luxurious apartment that has cost me zero dollars—it's free. Besides, its value now is three times the purchase price (which I do not add to my net worth).

Life is very comfortable in downtown Bangkok, all conveniences are nearby, specially schools for my children. We are now a big, happy family—me; my lovely Latin wife from Ecuador, Noemi Solorzano; my two beautiful children, Karan and Karuna; and my mother, Neela.

But we never know when crisis strikes again in one's journey. That is the nature of life. When I was about to finish writing this book, I had a motor-neuron scare. I could not move the fingers of my right hand when I get up in the morning. It would last only for a short time, and then it would go back to normal.

The thought of going down like my father made me anxious to finish and publish this book. For a moment, I thought that maybe I would have to end the book with a fourth crisis and a sad ending. Fortunately, that was not the case.

But even if the same condition falls upon me, the situation will be different from my father's. I've prepared all my life, should anything like that happen to me. Nobody knows what's going to happen. That's why we must secure our financial future to protect what is important to us—ourselves, our family, and our loved ones.

To protect the future of my family, I am constantly trying to increase my active income and continue to save and invest. Passive income and saving from active income both are being put into the process of doubling and compounding. When I predict my financial future, I am happy to see that I will easily achieve permanent financial freedom.

Being the sole breadwinner, I have also highly insured myself. I don't want to leave my family behind with debt when crisis strikes. I limit the leverage so that I can sleep well at night. Nothing crazy and greedy. Greed and leverage are best friends.

As both my active and passive incomes grow, so does my courage to buy bigger assets. In the future, I will sell small assets to buy bigger assets and continue to invest, grow, and *grow richer*.

To the reader, I really hope you've enjoyed traveling with me as I shared my life journey with you. My story was about a man crawling out of the middle-class trap and into financial freedom. As I've said earlier in the book, my goal was to share with you my simple money concepts that would lead you and your family into permanent financial freedom.

While property investment is the way I found it easiest to apply these concepts, there may be other equally viable options, depending on your life circumstances.

The concepts I've shared with you here are easily applied to other business and investment options. It was a bumpy road, filled with trials and challenges, but I hope the lessons I learned as I navigated my way through various crises will help you avoid some of the same struggles that I encountered.

Now that we've come to the end of this book, it's time for you to put the concepts you've learned into practice. Below is an exercise designed to help you predict your financial future.

In the "Predict Your Financial Future" chapter, you calculated how much money you can have by the age of sixty-three, based on your savings and investments. You have that figure in hand.

Now, let's see if that figure is going to be enough to make you financially free throughout your retirement.

Ask yourself, "What are the monthly expenses of my desired lifestyle now?" (If you know that you cannot afford your desired lifestyle because you have billionaire tastes, at least consider what expenses are necessary to sustain your current lifestyle.)

Then note them down, and add them up.

Once you have that figure, check for the rate of inflation in your country. A quick online search will tell you what it is. You can use the average inflation rate over a large period.

Once you know the rate of inflation in your country, use the rule of 72 to calculate how many years it will take for inflation to double in your country, and plot the doubling chart for your lifestyle expenses as shown in the earlier chapter.

My monthly expenses today:_____

The rate of inflation:_____

My Expenses will double in : _____ years.

Doubling Chart of Your Lifestyle Expenses with---------Percent Inflation

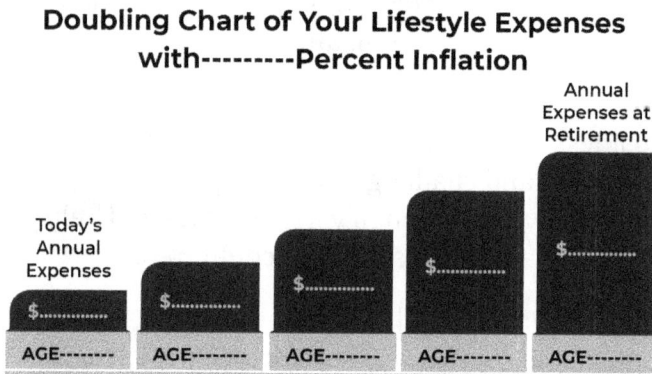

What will your monthly expenses look like by the time you are sixty-three? Is your passive income at sixty-three higher than your expenses? Will you be financially free when you retire? If not, are there things you can change today that will put you on the path to financial freedom?

Will this passive income be enough to beat inflation and sustain you through your retirement? If not, it is wise to make some changes ahead of time. You have all the keys and equipment necessary to beat the big boss. Start today!

Find a way to increase your active income, save more, buy fewer liabilities and more assets, simplify your life, invest maximum money at the highest rate possible, and invest for passive income and positive cash flow.

Do all you can to have only good debt. I know each of these things seem difficult, but as you tackle each one individually and move ahead, step by step, you will succeed!

Also, never forget to enjoy the present! This time will never come again. I wish you many blessings in your life as you all move towards a bright future!

Appendix

A.1 Compounding

For those of you who would like to look at the concept of compounding in more detail, I would add in some further examples. Maybe some of you are still not sure what compounding even is. It's very important to understand, so I am going to explain it as simply as I can.

Let's start with an example. If you deposit $10,000 in your local bank for seven years at a rate of 10 percent per annum, what is the amount you will receive after seven years? That's $10,000 + $7,000 = $17,000, right?

But wait! There are two ways to calculate the final amount you will receive after seven years. You could calculate it by using simple interest or compounded interest.

Simple Interest Calculation

$10,000 x 10% = $1,000 is interest for 1 year

$1,000 x 7 years = $7,000 is interest for 7 years

So, after seven years you will receive your investment of $10,000, plus the interest of $7,000 for seven years, making a total of $17,000.

But if you can compound the interest, you will find how quickly your money can grow.

Compound Interest Calculation

Year 1

$10,000 x 10% = $1,000 interest for the 1st year

Invest and Grow Rich

So, after one year, your money will become $10,000 + $1000 = $11,000. For the second year, your interest will be based in the new amount in your account, $11,000.

Year 2

$11,000 x 10% = $1,100 interest for the 2nd year

$11,000 + $1,100 = $12,100

Year 3

$12,100 x 10% = $1,210 interest for the 3rd year

$12,100 + $1,210 = $13,310

Year 4

$13,310 x 10% = $1,331 interest for the 4th year

$13,310 + $1,331 = $14,641

Year 5

$14,641 x 10% = $1,464.10 interest for the 5th year

$14,641 + $1,464.10 = $16,105.10

Year 6

$16,105.1 x 10% = $1,610.51 interest for the 6th year

$16,105.10 + $1,610.51 = $17,715.61

Year 7

$17,715.61 x 10% = $1,771.56 interest for the 7th year

So, at the end of the 7th year, your money will become $17,715.61 + $1,771,56 = $19,487.17.

Simple interest will you get $17,000 after seven years, but by compound interest calculations, you will receive $19,487.17 after seven years. This is the magic of compounding! It looks like a small difference, but if you keep on doing it for many more years, in the long term, this difference becomes very big, just like what we saw with our doubling chart in chapter 2, which starts from just a dollar and goes until you have over a billion dollars. The fight and struggle is for this difference.

It's also interesting to note that the above compounding interest calculations prove the rule of 72. You have invested $10,000 at a compounded rate of 10 percent with the bank. Rule of 72 says that if the compounding rate of return is 10 percent, then you can double your money in around seven years (72/10 = 7.20).

You can see that after seven years, you have got an amount of $19,487.17, and in another two months, you will have $19,811.00, which is quite close to $20,000, which is double of $10,000 that you originally invested. Since the rule of 72 works, we use it for easier calculations.

A.2 **The Rate of Return**

The rate of return is simply the profit you make on your investment per year. The simplest way of understanding the rate of return is going over your savings account. If you deposit $10,000 into your savings account and receive 5 percent interest per annum, then your rate of return is 5 percent.

In the case of rental properties, if you buy a property valued at $100,000 and rent it out at a net monthly rate of $1000, that would be a 12 percent return on the value of the property ($1000 per month means $12,000 per year).

$100,000 x 12% = $12,000

So, if you are receiving a net monthly rental income of $1000 on your $100,000 property, then it's a 12 percent return per annum.

If you receive a net monthly rental income of only $800 on this property, then your rate of return is only 9.6 percent.

$100,000 x 9.6% = $9600 ($800 x 12 months = $9,600)

Below I have included a formula to calculate the rate of return on rental properties.

Rate of Return = Monthly Rent x 1200 / Value of Property

Take the monthly rent you are receiving, multiply by 1200, and then divide by the value of the property to get the rate of return.

I hope these explanations have helped you get a grasp of these concepts. I am excited for you as you plan for your financial freedom. Good luck!

www.ingramcontent.com/pod-product-compliance
Lightning Source LLC
Chambersburg PA
CBHW071418210326
41597CB00020B/3554